Happy Cooking!

Betty Groff

Betty Groff's Up-Home Down-Home Cookbook

by

BETTY GROFF

Designed by Flat Tulip Studio
Illustrated by Thomas M. Wise

Coordinator — Barbara Adams

GFE
POND PRESS

650 Pinkerton Road
Mount Joy, Pennsylvania, 17552

Books by Betty Groff

GOOD EARTH AND COUNTRY COOKING
BETTY GROFF'S COUNTRY GOODNESS COOKBOOK
BETTY GROFF'S UP-HOME DOWN-HOME COOKBOOK

Designed by FLAT TULIP STUDIO

FIRST EDITION

Library of Congress Cataloging in Publication Data

Groff, Betty
Betty Groff's Up-Home Down-Home Cookbook

Includes index
1. Cookery, American   2. Cookery, Pennsylvania Dutch
I. Title.   II. Title:
Betty Groff's Up-Home Down-Home Cookbook

ISBN: 0-943395-01-1
Library of Congress Catalog Card Number 87-090593
Copyright © 1987
Printed in the UNITED STATES OF AMERICA

To my Dad, Clarence N. Herr. Your compassion, love and laughter keep me going. Your exemplary life has given many the encouragement to reach higher goals. My love and respect for you can never be put in words, but only shared with others as I share.

Contents

The recipes in this book will serve 4 to 6, unless otherwise stated.

UP-HOME DOWN-HOME

The sharing of food has always been a sign of love and hospitality in Lancaster County, the heart of Pennsylvania's famous Dutch Country and home of the state's best known country cook, Betty Groff.

Long before Tex-Mex and Cajun became trendy bywords of regional cuisine, Betty was building her reputation by serving such hearty Pennsylvania favorites as chow chow, baked ham, dried corn and shoofly pie at Groff's Farm Restaurant.

Culinary greats Craig Claiborne and the late James Beard "discovered" her nearly 25 years ago when she served Saturday-night dinners to tourists as a way of meeting people. Since then, she has treated hundreds of thousands of visitors from all over the world to a taste of her wit and her brand of good cooking at the Farm and at the Groff's historic Cameron Estate Inn.

No one forgets meeting Betty, perhaps because she isn't at all like the picture one envisions. Far from being an apron-wearing, bespectacled and sun-bonneted grandma who hasn't left the farm since the horse went lame, she is a thoroughly modern businesswoman who drives a red Corvette and keeps a trim figure that belies the plump Pennsylvania Dutch stereotype. When people ask her how she manages to stay slim, she quips that she's been through a calorie zapper. Fact of the matter is that she could eat like a farmhand and never gain an ounce because she's never still long enough for calories to catch up with her.

Nouvelle cuisine never suited Betty. It was too far removed from the food traditions she cherished. While the rest of the world was trying to like such exotic combinations as blank and blank, she had already begun making the move from the hearty fare of her past to what is now being called the "New American Cuisine".

She takes the finest and freshest of the state's abundant produce, stirs in her experiences from traveling and teaching and adds her interpretation of the past to serve Pennsylvania fare that's better than ever.

Betty has tucked it all into the pages of this cookbook that's brimming with new recipes, ideas for natural seasonings, tips on lighter and healthier cooking, time-saving techniques, microwave cooking times and culinary hints.

She makes no pretense about the foods she offers because that's not her style. After all, anyone who pickles watermelon rind and enjoys a good meal of stuffed pig's stomach isn't going to create recipes requiring high-priced, exotic ingredients.

Betty mixes in some philosophy, too, when she says, "People should cook what they like for guests, friends, and family rather than what they think they ought to cook to be trendy. Serving foods from your past means you're sharing a part of yourself with them."

That's why she never loses sight of the flavor of her own roots that go back ten generations to Lancaster County's first settlers. She includes her trademark dish, Chicken Stoltzfus, and the second most popular dish ever served at the Farm — her son Charlie's country-good potato salad. She says "These recipes are like teddy bears. Just having them around makes me feel good."

Unlike secretive cooks who refuse to share recipes, Betty gives of hers freely, based on the wisdom of James Beard who once told her, "You can give the same recipe to four people and the dish will turn out differently for each one."

Part missionary and part coach when she's writing or teaching in the kitchen, she cajoles cooks with such homey advice as, "Foods talk to you if you learn to listen. If you're baking pie pastry in the oven and don't know if it's done in the center, listen to it. If you hear ticking, it needs a little more time."

Mindful that many of her happiest childhood memories are associated with food, Betty uses subtle, Tom-Sawyer-style persuasion to encourage families to cook and work together. It's an idea that has worked for her because the Groff family, including her husband Abe, son, daughter-in-law and grandchildren spend much of their time together cooking up new ideas for the Farm Restaurant and the Cameron Estate Inn.

The enthusiasm is contagious. Anyone who listens to Betty or spends a few minutes browsing through what she writes could wind up in the kitchen trying out recipes faster than a brush can be dipped in whitewash.

1

APPETIZERS & BREADS

APPETIZERS & BREADS

Pennsylvania leads the country in the production of potato chips and pretzels, but that's just the beginning of our snack food repertoire.

Simple oyster crackers, seasoned with butter-flavored oil and dried dill go well with conversation though they're sure to be gone before you've finished talking.

Stuffed mushroom caps, quick cheese spread, fried cheese, soft pretzels and broiled meat spread will take a bit more time and work.

But funnel cakes are the real test, particularly if you're trying to make them picture-perfect. I know because I must have made at least 300 (a conservative estimate) for an all-day and practically all-night CHOCOLATIER Magazine photo session.

Funnel cakes are, of course, our version of fried dough that's sprinkled with powdered sugar and served warm. My recipe, developed originally for the magazine, contains the added flavoring from mini chips that bubble to the surface and leave a trickle of chocolate wherever they melt.

I've watched people make simple round crullers of fried dough at the New York State Fair, but they're bland and ordinary to those of us who have turned funnel cake making into an art.

First, the batter is poured into a funnel. Be sure the throat of the funnel is wide enough to allow the mini chips to pass through. The cook must keep a finger over the opening until ready to release the ribbon of batter into the frying pan of hot fat.

The challenge is releasing the batter in one continuous motion, working from the center to the outer part of the pan, to produce concentric rings that fill the pan. The motion must be continuous or there will be breaks in the rings and the fat temperature must be right or the dough will be soggy and greasy rather than light and crisp.

The day I spent making funnel cakes for the magazine photographs was long. We finally achieved perfection — the ultimate funnel cake — at midnight. I'd managed to make six complete rings in the frying pan and the photographer was satisfied with the picture. I was overjoyed because I felt like I could have slipped through the funnel myself and pulled him through after me!

The funnel cakes, along with snails and sugar pies made from baking scraps, were occasional snacks, but breads were our every-day staples.

My mother baked bread at least two or three times a week and early on, I was there to help. My first culinary memory is the smell of that freshly baked bread scenting the air in the early morning. A warm slice, spread with fresh farm butter, with cottage

cheese and apple butter, or with egg cheese and molasses, was heavenly eating. I always earned a slice or two by taking on the heavy responsibility of making sure no drafts affected the bread's rising.

As I grew older, I marveled at how the yeast grew and made the bread rise and came to appreciate that a cook never conquers yeast baking. Although a pie will always turn out the same, every loaf of bread, like each snowflake, is a little bit different.

There was a lot of other baking done on the farm besides loaf after loaf of white or whole wheat. Corn bread, actually called corn pone, was one of my favorites. In June, when the sour cherries were ripe, they were sugared and spooned over the corn bread to achieve something that was similar to, but not as sweet as, strawberry shortcake. Sometimes, we even floured extra cherries and put them right in the batter.

Cloud biscuits so light they practically float, Oomph bread so heavy with nutritious grains that one slice will bowl you over and yeast rolls with golden flecks of cheese, are more modern recipes that still promise plenty of old-time flavor.

No one has to bake breads any more but working with them is good therapy and more importantly, the accompanying aroma and taste will tell the family how much you care.

LISA'S HAM AND CHEESE BUNS

Served warm, they're unbelievable!

Dissolve yeast in warm water in large mixing bowl. Add sugar, salt, egg, shortening and 1 cup flour. Beat at low speed until well blended. Add remaining cup of flour. Blend and scrape batter from side of bowl. Cover with cloth and let rise in warm, draft-free place until doubled, about 30 minutes.

Grease 12 medium muffin cups. Dice prepared ham and divide into twelve, if you prefer to place ham on top. If desired, fold the ham into batter. Stir down batter by beating twenty-five strokes. Spoon into muffin cups. Press 1 cheese cube into center of batter in each cup, making sure cheese is covered. Cover with cloth and let rise until batter reaches top of cups. Preheat oven to 350° F. Bake about 12 minutes. Serve warm.

Makes 1 dozen

1 package dry yeast
¾ cup warm water
2 Tablespoons sugar
1 teaspoon salt
1 egg
2 Tablespoons shortening
2 cups flour, divided
4 to 6 slices ham, diced, approximately 1 cup
½ teaspoon celery seed
½ teaspoon chives, chopped
1½ ounces sharp, colby or Swiss cheese, cubed into ½" pieces

STUFFED MUSHROOMS

Break the stems from the caps and measure out 1 cup. Blend the rest of the ingredients in a blender or food processor and fill the caps with the mixture. Bake in a preheated 350° F. oven for 15 minutes and serve warm.

Makes 24

24	medium sized mushrooms
⅓	cup chopped onions
⅓	cup celery
2	Tablespoons parsley
¼	green pepper, chopped
⅓	cup cream cheese
¾	cup fresh bread crumbs

MARINATED MUSHROOMS

Combine the first seven ingredients in a small saucepan and bring to a boil. Add the mushrooms and simmer for 10 minutes. Let cool, and chill in a covered bowl overnight.

⅓	cup red wine vinegar
1	small onion, sliced thin and separated into rings
1	teaspoon prepared mustard
⅓	cup salad oil
1	teaspoon salt
2	teaspoons dried parsley flakes
1	Tablespoon brown sugar
1	pound fresh mushrooms

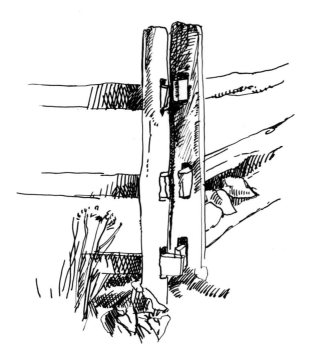

FRIED CHEESE

Cut the cheese into 24 sticks or slices. Dip each piece into the beaten egg, then into the crumbs and seeds. Repeat the process again and chill for an hour. Drop into a deep fryer or a skillet with an inch of oil in it and cook for a couple minutes until lightly browned. Drain on absorbent paper and serve hot.

Makes 18–24 sticks or slices

12 ounce package cheddar cheese
2 eggs, lightly beaten
¾ cups dried bread crumbs
2 Tablespoons sesame seeds
Oil for frying

SNAILS

A favorite snack, snails were made from leftover dough from pie baking. Another example of how everything was used to its best advantage.

Moisten leftover pie dough with a sprinkle of water. Dust with flour and roll ¼" thick. Spread with melted butter or margarine. Sprinkle with cinnamon and sugar or jelly and roll up like a jelly roll. Cut in ½" slices. Place on greased baking sheet and bake in a 350° F. oven for 15 minutes. Serve plain, buttered, or with butter icing on top.

VARIATION

Grated cheddar or herb cheese may be substituted.

OYSTER CRACKER NIBBLES

You can't eat just one!

Mix all of the ingredients together, making sure that the crackers are well coated and oiled. Allow the mixture to stand for four hours, stirring occasionally from the bottom.

1 13–16 ounce package oyster crackers, tiny size

1 envelope ranch style dressing mix, dry

¾ cup butter flavored popping oil

BASIC WHITE BREAD

Cool the milk. When it is lukewarm, add the sugar, salt, and butter. Let the yeast proof (form tiny bubbles on the surface, which shows it is active) and add it to the milk. Combine with the flour and mix thoroughly. Knead vigorously on a lightly floured surface or in an electric mixer with a dough hook, until the dough is smooth and elastic to the touch. Put the dough in a greased bowl, turning it so it is oily on all sides. A vegetable cooking spray may be used. Cover with a damp cloth and let it rise in a warm, draft-free spot until doubled in bulk. Cut or punch the dough and knead a little more. Divide the dough into 3 parts. Shape each piece into a smooth loaf and place in a greased loaf pan. Cover with a cloth. Let the dough rise in a warm place until doubled in bulk. Bake in a preheated 350° F. oven for 45 minutes until the bread pulls away from the sides of the pan. Brush the top of the loaves with the melted butter.

Makes 3 loaves, 5″ x 11″ each

- 2 cups scalded milk
- 3 Tablespoons granulated sugar
- 1¼ Tablespoons salt
- 3 Tablespoons butter
- 2 packages dry granular yeast or 2 yeast cakes dissolved in ¼ cup lukewarm water (110° F.)
- 7 cups sifted all-purpose flour, or stone ground flour, if available

Melted butter

BASIC WHOLE WHEAT BREAD

Use Basic White Bread recipe substituting whole wheat flour for ½ of the white flour. Add ¼ cup honey to the milk mixture.

MEAL BREAD

It's good all by itself!

Soften the yeast in the lukewarm water. Combine the cornmeal, brown sugar, salt, boiling water and oil in a large mixing bowl and blend. Add the yeast, whole wheat, and rye flour and 2 cups of the unbleached flour to the mixture gradually and beat with the mixer until the batter is smooth. Add 2 to 2½ cups unbleached flour by hand until you can work with the dough. Knead on a lightly floured surface until smooth and elastic. Place the dough in a greased bowl, turning it over once to grease the top. Cover with a cloth and let rise in a warm, draft-free place until it's doubled in bulk — about an hour. Punch down, and let dough rest, covered, for 10 minutes. Shape into two loaves and put into greased loaf pans. Cover and let rise until double, about 30 minutes. Bake in a preheated 425° F. oven for 30 minutes or until the loaf sounds hollow when tapped on top and is golden brown. Remove from the pans and cool on a rack. This bread is delicious toasted.

Makes 2 loaves

2   packages dry yeast
½   cup water, lukewarm
½   cup yellow cornmeal
⅓   cup brown sugar
2   teaspoons salt
2   cups boiling water
¼   cup peanut oil
¾   cup whole wheat flour
½   cup rye flour
4 to 4½   cups unbleached flour

DILL BREAD

Soften the yeast in the warm water. Combine the cottage cheese (which has been heated to lukewarm), sugar, dill weed, chives, butter, salt, soda, egg and yeast in a mixing bowl and gradually add the flour to form a stiff dough. Scrape the sides of the bowl several times during the additions of flour. Cover with a cloth and let rise in a warm, draft-free place until doubled in bulk, about an hour. Punch down and knead, shaping into either a round or loaf shape. Place in a well greased casserole or loaf pan and allow to rise again for 30 to 40 minutes. Bake in a preheated 350° F. oven for 40 minutes or until the loaf is golden brown. Place pan on a rack and allow the bread to cool for about 15 minutes before removing from the pan.

Makes 1 loaf

1 package dry yeast
¼ cup water, lukewarm
2 Tablespoons sugar
1 cup creamed cottage cheese
1 teaspoon dill weed or dill seed
1 Tablespoon chives, freeze-dried
1 Tablespoon butter
1 teaspoon onion salt
¼ teaspoon baking soda
1 egg, lightly beaten
2¼ to 2½ cups all purpose flour
1 teaspoon butter, to grease top of baked loaf

GLAZED LEMON BREAD

Mix the eggs, sugar, shortening, lemon juice and rind together and add the milk. Sift the baking powder, salt and flour together and stir into the batter. Fold the nuts into the mixture and pour into a loaf pan that has been lined with foil and greased. Bake in a preheated 350° F. oven for 50–60 minutes. Mix the sugar and lemon juice together in a small saucepan and heat over medium heat, stirring until the sugar dissolves. Pour over the bread while the loaf is still hot. Let stand until cool and remove from the foil. Wrap in wax paper or plastic wrap and chill thoroughly.

2 eggs, beaten
1 cup sugar
6 Tablespoons shortening
1 lemon, juice and grated rind
½ cup milk
1 teaspoon baking powder
¼ teaspoon salt
1½ cups flour
½ cup chopped pecans

GLAZE
½ cup sugar
Juice from 1 lemon

KATHY'S REAL OOMPH BREAD

Dissolve yeast in ½ cup water. Combine 2 cups flour, salt, molasses, butter, egg and 1 cup water in mixer until smooth (approximately 2 minutes). Add yeast mixture, wheat germ and remaining cup of flour and mix until smooth, (approximately 2 minutes.) Place in a greased 1½ quart casserole. Brush or spray with oil. Cover with damp cloth and let rise in a warm, draft-free place until doubled in bulk. Bake in a preheated oven at 375° F. on lowest rack, for 50 to 60 minutes. Cover top of bread with foil for the last 10 minutes or as soon as it is the desired browness.

1 package dry granular yeast
½ cup lukewarm water
3 cups all-purpose flour
2 teaspoons salt
3 Tablespoons light molasses
2 Tablespoons soft butter
1 egg
1 cup warm water
1 cup wheat germ
Oil or vegetable spray for baking dish

VARIATION

Stir in 1 cup of any garden vegetable, grated or finely chopped, plus herbs of your choice such as parsley, chives or chervil.

CHEESE SPREAD

Grind cheese in blender or food processor and add the eggs. Chop the onion and green pepper fine and mix with the mayonnaise. Blend everything together. The mixture should spread well. If necessary add more mayonnaise.

Makes 3 cups

12 ounces sharp cheddar cheese
⅓ cup green pepper
2 green onions, including tops
3 eggs, hard boiled and peeled
⅓ cup mayonnaise

BOLOGNA SPREAD

This is an excellent summer spread or dip. Served warm, it's great on toast, rye or party crackers.

Blend thoroughly in a mixer or food processor.

- 1 cup bologna, finely ground
- ½ cup cream cheese
- ¼ cup mayonnaise
- ½ teaspoon coarsely ground pepper
- ¼ cup pickle relish
- ◆ Dash of tabasco

ICE BOX ROLLS

A real time saver. Make the dough one day, bake the rolls the next.

Pour boiling water over the shortening, sugar and salt. Blend together and cool. Dissolve the yeast in the lukewarm water. Mix the shortening mixture, yeast and eggs, and slowly add the flour and stir until well blended. Place in the refrigerator to rise overnight. Punch down the dough and either roll out or cut and shape as desired. Let rise again about an hour before baking in a preheated 400° F. oven for 15 minutes, or until golden brown.

Yields about 5 dozen rolls

- 1 cup shortening
- ¾ cup sugar
- 2 teaspoons salt
- 2 eggs, lightly beaten
- 2 packages dry yeast
- 1 cup boiling water
- 1 cup lukewarm water
- 6 cups all purpose flour, unsifted

MUMSIE'S MUFFINS

Barb's grandmother Grace Knepper, Mumsie, was "the lady everyone loved". An excellent cook, she provided the teachers from the Alfarata Elementary School a hot lunch each day for a pittance. She supervised her church kitchen as wife of a well-known minister and insurance agent. Her grandfather, Lewis, always said, "We insure people for this life and the next".

Sift the dry ingredients and blend with the liquid and the egg. Fold in the melted shortening and stir until well blended. Fill well greased muffin cups half full and bake in a preheated oven at 400° F. for 20 minutes or until lightly browned.

2	cups flour, sifted
1	teaspoon salt
1	Tablespoon sugar
4	teaspoons baking powder
1	egg, lightly beaten
1	cup milk or water
4	Tablespoons shortening, melted

VARIATIONS

BLUEBERRY MUFFINS — Add 1 scant cup of blueberries, washed, drained, and rolled in flour. Add sugar if berries are not very sweet. CHEESE MUFFINS — Add 4 Tablespoons grated cheddar cheese and a dash of paprika. Top with grated cheese. DATE MUFFINS — Add ½ cup of finely cut, unsweetened dates and flavor with vanilla. HOLIDAY MUFFINS — Add ½ cup of finely cut mixed dried fruits.

Makes 16 average or 24 small muffins.

GOLDEN CORN GEMS

Sift together the corn meal, flour, sugar, baking powder and salt. Cream the shortening and beat in the egg. Add the dry ingredients alternately with milk. Do not overbeat. Pour into greased corn bread molds, muffin tins or baking dish. Bake in preheated oven at 375° F. for 20 to 25 minutes or until golden brown.

Makes 12

1	cup yellow cornmeal
1	cup all-purpose flour
¼	cup sugar
2	teaspoons baking powder
½	teaspoon salt
3	Tablespoons shortening
1	egg
1	cup sour milk (buttermilk could be used)

CLOUD BISCUITS

Light as a feather!

Mix flour, sugar, baking powder and salt. Cut in shortening with fork or pastry blender. Stir in the egg and milk, mixing thoroughly. Knead lightly on a floured surface and pat or roll to about ¾" thick. Cut in desired shapes and place on ungreased baking sheet. Dip small sugar cubes in orange juice and press lightly into top of each biscuit. Bake in preheated 400° F. oven for 12 to 14 minutes or until lightly browned. Serve warm.

2	cups flour
1	Tablespoon sugar
4	teaspoons baking powder
½	teaspoon salt
½	cup shortening
1	egg, lightly beaten
⅔	cup milk (buttermilk is best)
16	sugar cubes (optional)
¼	cup orange juice (optional)

VARIATIONS

Top biscuits with ½ cup grated cheese. Brush tops with melted butter and sprinkle with cinnamon sugar.

Makes 16 biscuits

BERTHA'S WAFFLES

Beat egg yolks until light in color. Sift the dry ingredients together. Add the milk and melted butter to the beaten egg yolks. Slowly add the dry ingredients and beat until smooth. Beat the egg whites until stiff and fold them into the batter last. Pour about ¾ cup of batter on the grill for each waffle.

2	cups flour
1	teaspoon salt
2	eggs, separated
2	cups milk
3½	teaspoons baking powder
4	Tablespoons butter, melted

Makes about 6 medium waffles

CORNMEAL GRIDDLE CAKES

Pour boiling water over the cornmeal and stir. Allow the mixture to cool a little and add the molasses, milk and the egg. Stir in the dry ingredients which have been sifted together. The batter will be thin. Pour about ¼ cup batter for each cake onto a hot griddle. When the bubbles break and the top of the cake looks dry it can be flipped over.

Yields 8 medium griddle cakes

1 cup cornmeal
½ cup boiling water
1 Tablespoon molasses
1 egg, lightly beaten
1 cup milk
4 Tablespoons flour
3 teaspoons baking powder
⅔ teaspoon salt

CHOCOHOLICS' FUNNEL CAKES

Quite unusual, but so simple to make and definitely a "memory food."

Blend dry ingredients. Add beaten egg and milk, stirring until smooth. Fold in grated chocolate, mini morsels or chips and pour into pitcher or funnel. In heavy skillet, pour oil ⅓" deep and heat oil to 390° F. Pour thin stream of batter from funnel or pitcher in form of circle — starting in center, circling, but not stopping until you get desired size. Fry until golden brown. With a fork in each hand, gently turn and fry until golden on opposite side. Remove and drain on paper towels. Serve immediately while they are warm with powdered sugar for dipping.

1 cup unsifted flour
2 teaspoons granulated sugar
1 teaspoon baking powder
½ teaspoon salt
1 egg, lightly beaten
¾ cup milk
3 ounces grated chocolate (approximately ⅓ cup, mini-morsels or chips)
Oil for frying

BLUEBERRY PANCAKES

Sift together the flour, baking powder, salt and sugar. Blend eggs, milk, sour cream and butter in a separate bowl. Pour liquids over dry ingredients. Mix lightly until blended. Do not mix any longer than necessary, as extra mixing will toughen the pancakes. Gently fold in the blueberries. Fry on a hot buttered or oiled griddle or in a heavy skillet.

Serves 6

1½	**cups sifted flour**
4	**teaspoons baking powder**
½	**teaspoon salt**
1½	**Tablespoons sugar**
2	**eggs**
1¼	**cups milk**
⅓	**cup sour cream**
3	**Tablespoons soft butter**
¾	**cup blueberries**

HINT: Shake the rinsed blueberries in a little of the flour mixture in a plastic or paper bag to coat them before adding them to the batter. This will help them stay whole.

BLUEBERRY SYRUP

This is marvelous on anything you like to have syrup on, but I suggest using it with the Blueberry Pancakes for a real blueberry treat!

Stir sugar, nutmeg, lemon juice and water until dissolved. Bring to boil and add blueberries. Simmer for 15 minutes. Strain if desired.

Makes 5 cups

1	**cup granulated sugar**
¼	**teaspoon ground nutmeg**
1	**Tablespoon lemon juice**
1	**cup water**
4	**cups blueberries, well cleaned**

POTATO BREAD

In a large bowl, combine the sugar, salt, yeast and 1½ cups of the flour. In a large saucepan, mix the water, mashed potatoes and milk. Add butter or margarine and heat over low heat until very warm, stirring often. Using the mixer on low speed, gradually beat the liquid into the dry ingredients just until blended. Beat in the eggs and 1 cup of flour, stopping often to scrape down the sides of the bowl. Continue mixing while adding the rest of the flour, enough to make a soft dough. Turn the dough onto a lightly floured board and knead until smooth and elastic. More flour may need to be worked into the dough. Shape into a ball and place in a large greased mixing bowl, turning the dough over so the top is greased. Cover and let rise in a warm, draft-free place until doubled in bulk, about 1 hour. Punch the dough down and cut it in half. After resting for 15 minutes, shape into a ball again and place in a well greased casserole. Cover and let rise again for an hour before baking. If you wish, cut two parallel slashes before the bread rises. Just before baking in a preheated 400° F. oven, brush the tops of the loaves with milk. Bake for 40 minutes or until browned and the loaves sound hollow when tapped. Remove from the casseroles immediately and let cool on racks.

Makes 2 round loaves

3	Tablespoons sugar
1	Tablespoon salt
2	packages active dry yeast (2 Tablespoons)
⅔	cup lukewarm water
1½	cups mashed potatoes
1	cup milk
¼	cup butter or margarine
3	eggs
7 to 8	cups all purpose flour, if using stone ground flour, use less

ZUCCHINI BREAD

Beat eggs until light and foamy. Add oil, sugar, grated zucchini and vanilla extract. Mix lightly, but thoroughly. Add flour, salt, soda, cinnamon, baking powder, nutmeg and cloves. Blend well and fold in nuts. Put into 2 greased loaf pans and bake in a preheated 350° F. oven for one hour.

Makes 2 loaves

3	eggs
1	cup salad oil
2	cups sugar
2	cups grated, peeled zucchini
3	teaspoons vanilla extract
3	cups flour, sifted
1	teaspoon salt
1	teaspoon baking soda
3	teaspoons cinnamon
½	teaspoon baking powder
½	teaspoon nutmeg
½	teaspoon ground cloves
1½	cups walnuts or almonds, chopped

2

CHEESE, EGGS, & NOODLES

CHEESE, EGGS & NOODLES

While some children earned summer spending money selling lemonade and cookies at sidewalk stands, noodles were my childhood "bread and butter." Whenever I needed extra cash for gifts, I made noodles to sell at my father's butcher shop or in the nearby village of Strasburg. Long after my friends had to close up shop for the season (the demand for ice-cold lemonade drops markedly in December and January), I was still in business. That's because noodles are to Pennsylvania Dutch households what pastas are to Italian families — year-round necessities.

Easy to make with a minimum of ingredients, the only significant expenditure in noodle making is one of time. But no matter whether you choose to make fresh egg noodles, spinach noodles or the large pot-pie squares, you'll find the taste well worth the effort. Homemade noodles are as different from dried, store-bought noodles as canned vegetables are from fresh ones.

These days, Abe and I will sometimes invite friends over for a night in the kitchen and alternate between making noodles and the sauces to go with them. But I've also made many a batch of noodles with the help of my children and grandchildren. Sometimes, we do it the old-fashioned way but more often, we use a pasta machine. My family loves watching the machine turn a small piece of dough into a large, thin sheet. I personally enjoy the therapeutic effects of rolling out noodles by hand.

A writer once compared my noodle making speed to the culinary acumen of a highly skilled Japanese chef whose knife-wielding ability enables him to dice foods faster than the eye can see. Although I'm not quite that fast, it doesn't take long for me to roll out the dough on a floured surface — particularly when I've had a tension-filled day.

Once the dough is in a thin rectangle, it is rolled, jelly-roll style, and sliced through at quarter-inch intervals. To separate the noodle rounds and open them up, I simply toss them in the air, as if I were playing an old-fashioned game of jacks. Allow the noodles to air-dry for a few minutes and they'll be ready for the cook pot.

I wouldn't want you to think I spent my whole childhood simply learning to make noodles. This chapter also contains the recipe for a cheese soufflé which was the first dish I made in Home Economics class. You'll also find my 4-H recipe for macaroni and cheese that took the place of our traditional bacon-and-egg Saturday morning breakfast for months. I was flattered that the family seemed to love the dish so much

until I found out the only reason they requested it was because it was the only thing they were sure I could make.

I felt like consoling myself with some egg cheese, an old-fashioned treat that was savored at any time of the day, from dawn breakfasts to bedtime snacks.

Made with eggs, milk, buttermilk, a pinch of salt and some sugar, the blend of ingredients was heated gently until it separated into curds and whey. (Could egg cheese have been the undoing of Little Miss Muffet?) The curds were spooned into pierced tin molds or coffee cans, baskets, sieves or colanders and allowed to drain until a smooth, soft-spreading cheese was formed.

When ready, the egg cheese resembles ricotta and can be substituted for it in lasagna. But it's at its best when smeared onto homemade bread and drizzled with molasses that'll make you sticky from ear to ear. Now that's a comfort food!

CHEESE SOUFFLÉ

This was one of my Home Economics favorites. Quick and easy, but always impressive to serve. Make sure your guests will be ready to be seated the minute it is pulled from the oven.

Butter bottom and sides of a 2½ quart soufflé dish or casserole. Dust with parmesan cheese. Melt butter and blend in flour, onion, mustard, salt and worcestershire sauce. Cook, stirring constantly, until smooth and bubbly. Gradually add milk and stir until thickened. Remove from heat and add cheese. Beat egg whites with cream of tartar until stiff but not dry. Beat yolks until fluffy and lemon colored. Stir cheese sauce into yolks, slowly. Gently fold mixture into beaten egg whites and pour into prepared soufflé dish. With back of serving spoon, circle one inch from edge to form a "top hat." Bake in preheated 350° F. oven for approximately 40 minutes or until delicately brown. It should pull away from the sides a bit but will shake slightly in center. Serve immediately.

Parmesan cheese for dusting casserole

- 3 **Tablespoons butter**
- 3 **Tablespoons flour**
- 1 **Tablespoon finely chopped onion**
- 1 **teaspoon prepared mustard**
- ½ **teaspoon salt**
- 1 **teaspoon worcestershire sauce**
- 1½ **cups milk**
- 1 **cup shredded cheddar cheese (4 ounces)**
- 6 **eggs, separated**
- ¼ **teaspoon cream of tartar**

MACARONI AND CHEESE

My old-fashioned stand-by.

Boil macaroni in 2 quarts of water seasoned with tiny pinch of saffron, salt and oil until tender, approximately 12 minutes. Drain and place in large mixing bowl. Stir in the cheeses, salt, pepper and milk. Blend thoroughly. Pour into a greased 2 quart baking dish and bake in preheated 375° F. oven for approximately 35 minutes, or until golden brown. Remove from oven and top with sliced olives and a few dashes of paprika.

MICROWAVE: Cover with plastic wrap and bake approximately 12 minutes.

8   ounces (2 cups) macaroni
◆ **Pinch of saffron**
½   teaspoon salt
1   Tablespoon butter or oil
½   cup sharp cheese, grated
1½   cups white American cheese, grated
⅓   teaspoon salt or salt substitute
½   teaspoon coarsely ground pepper
2   cups milk
◆ **Several dashes of paprika**
Sliced olives for topping (optional)

EGG CHEESE

I love to demonstrate this recipe because so few people ever see cheese being made "right before their eyes." It is so delicate and easy to make, approximately 12 minutes.

Warm the milk in a heavy or non-stick 4 quart pan. Beat the eggs until fluffy and add the buttermilk, salt, and sugar. Beat slightly and pour slowly into the warm milk. Cook several minutes on low heat, stirring occasionally with pierced or wooden spoon. Watch for the curds (the cheese) and whey to separate. As soon as the liquid becomes clear, remove the curds with a slotted spoon and gently place in mold. Make sure the mold is placed in a pan so the liquid can drain while cooling. The antique molds are priceless, but now the local tinsmiths are reproducing them. The piercing is done from the inside out so that as the cheese cools it takes the form of the piercing. A small, unpainted basket, sieve or colander with small holes may be substituted, but will not be as pretty when unmolded.

When cold and drained, unmold the cheese onto a cheese plate. Serve with bread and a drizzle of light molasses.

VARIATION

Some folks like to serve the cheese with fresh fruit. A dash of nutmeg gives it an added touch. This egg cheese may be used as a substitute for ricotta.

Makes 3 cheeses — Serves approximately 12

2 **quarts milk**
6 **eggs**
2 **cups buttermilk**
1 **teaspoon salt**
2 **teaspoons sugar**

CHEESE BLINTZES

Making the crepes ahead of time will be a big time saver! Prepare the crepes and freeze between wax paper.

Drain cottage cheese in strainer or colander for at least 30 minutes. If using egg cheese, there is no need of draining. Gently press out any excess liquid with back of spoon. In a bowl, mix cottage cheese with egg yolk, sugar and lemon juice. Spoon filling onto center of cooked crepes. Fold over bottom, both sides, and top as in a fat envelope. Melt butter in skillet and brown blintzes on both sides. Sprinkle with powdered sugar. Serve warm with sour cream and your favorite preserves.

Makes 12 to 14 blintzes

12 to 14 cooked crepes
2 cups small curd cottage cheese or egg cheese
1 egg yolk
2 Tablespoons sugar
1 Tablespoon lemon juice
2 Tablespoons butter
Powdered sugar
Dairy sour cream
Preserves

HAM AND CHEESE CREPES

They won't believe how simple this show-stopper is to prepare, so don't tell them!

Spread cooked crepes generously with sour cream. Lay 2 slices of ham across the center of each crepe and top with cheddar. Overlap the ends, turn over and place seam side down in 9″ x 13″ baking dish. Drizzle with melted butter and paprika and bake in a preheated 400° F. oven for 15 minutes or until slightly golden.

Basic Crepe Recipe, see Index
1 pound lean sliced, cooked ham, more or less if desired
10½ ounces sharp, yellow cheddar cheese, grated
1 pint sour cream
¼ cup melted butter
◆ Dash of paprika (optional)

BASIC CREPES

For dessert crepe, add 2 Tablespoons granulated sugar and ½ teaspoon of lemon extract.

Combine all ingredients except salad oil in large mixing bowl. Cover and refrigerate overnight or for several hours. When ready to make the crepes, season the crepe pan by adding the salad oil and heating the pan until it smokes. Remove pan from heat and sprinkle with salt. Wipe with paper towel and pan is ready to use. Pour ¼ cup of the batter into the heated pan. Cook over medium heat and turn when light or very pale brown, depending on how you plan to use the crepes.

HINT: Letting the batter stand overnight is the secret to tender crepes.

Makes 12–14 crepes

1 cup flour, sifted
3 eggs
½ teaspoon salt
½ cup beer
¾ cup milk
¼ cup water
2 Tablespoons melted butter
1 Tablespoon salad oil
Serving fillers (optional)
Lemon juice and powdered sugar
Honey
Your favorite jam or jelly

SAUSAGE AND CHEESE CASSEROLE

Barb uses this delicious time-saver for brunch or light suppers.

Place bread in greased 9″ x 13″ baking dish. You may trim the crusts if desired. Distribute sausage over bread. Place eggs, mustard, worcestershire sauce and milk in bowl and blend. Sprinkle grated cheeses over sausage and cover with milk mixture. Cover with plastic wrap and allow to sit in the refrigerator overnight. Bake in preheated 350° F. oven for 30 minutes or until top is golden brown.

6 to 8 slices firm white, day-old bread
1½ pounds mild flavored sausage, cooked and drained
4 eggs
1 teaspoon dijon mustard
1 teaspoon worcestershire sauce
2 cups milk
¾ cup sharp cheddar cheese, grated
¾ cup Swiss cheese, grated

DAVE'S BASIC CHEESE SAUCE

Our Chef at the Farm uses this sauce nearly every day. It's a complement to any fresh, crunchy vegetable.

Simmer chicken stock, onion, celery and basil for 20 minutes. Stir cornstarch into milk and add to above to thicken. Add grated cheese and stir until smooth.

Makes approximately 4 cups

3 cups chicken stock
1 Tablespoon minced onion
1 Tablespoon minced celery
½ teaspoon minced fresh basil (if dried, ¼ teaspoon)
4 Tablespoons cornstarch
½ cup cold milk
10 ounces yellow cheddar cheese, grated

JOHN'S BAKED EGGS

John and I shared many favorite recipes during breaks of the Nationwide Life Insurance Company board of directors' meetings. This is one I use quite often.

Place muffin halves in buttered or oiled baking dish. Place a slice of ham and tomato on each muffin. Break each egg into a cup and place on top of tomato. If you have a problem with the egg slipping off, use a spoon to form a cup in the center of the tomato slice. Mix the mustard, salt, cream, worcestershire and tabasco thoroughly and pour over the eggs. Top with grated cheese and dot each one with butter. Bake in pre-heated 350° F. oven for 20 minutes. Serve immediately.

Serves 4

4 **English muffins, split in half**

8 **slices of baked ham or Canadian bacon**

8 **slices of tomato**

8 **eggs**

1 **teaspoon dry mustard**

½ **teaspoon salt, less if ham is salty**

¾ **cup cream, ½ cup milk if you're watching calories**

1½ **teaspoons worcestershire sauce**

◆ **Dash of tabasco**

¾ **cup cheddar cheese, grated**

2 **Tablespoons butter (optional)**

RED DEVILED EGGS

Red beet eggs are a Pennsylvania Dutch tradition. Used on one of my PM Magazine segments, this recipe was requested by many viewers.

Cut beet eggs in half with sharp, clean knife. Remove the yolks and blend all the ingredients until smooth. Place in pastry tube and swirl the yolk mixture into the red eggs.

To make pickled beet juice: Add ½ cup sugar, ½ cup vinegar, ½ teaspoon salt and a dash of pepper to the juice drained from 2 16 ounce cans of beets.

12 **eggs, hard boiled and marinated in pickled beet juice for at least 10 hours**
¾ **cup mayonnaise**
1 **Tablespoon Pommery mustard**
1 **teaspoon salt**
1 **Tablespoon fresh parsley, minced**
¼ **cup sour cream**

CHARLIE'S EGGS BENEDICT

Charlie's secret to fine poached eggs is the vinegar in the water.

Toast English muffin halves. Broil or pan fry ham slices and place on muffin halves. Keep warm. Bring water, salt and vinegar to a boil and poach the eggs to desired doneness. Place on muffins and top with hollandaise sauce, see Index. Garnish with quarter slice of olive and chopped parsley.

1 quart water
1 Tablespoon salt
1 Tablespoon vinegar
4 eggs
2 English muffins — split
4 slices of ham, 2 ounces each
1 black olive, quartered
1 teaspoon chopped parsley
Hollandaise Sauce, see Index

BREAKFAST SOUFFLÉ

A time-saving recipe for easy entertaining.

Remove the crusts from the bread and butter on both sides. Cut in small cubes and place half of them in 8″ x 8″ baking dish. Sprinkle half of the grated cheese over the bread. Chop the dried beef coarsely and place over cheese. In a bowl, lightly whip eggs and add milk, mustard, salt and pepper. Pour half of mixture over the above. Add the remaining bread cubes and milk mixture and top with the remaining cheese. Refrigerate overnight. Remove soufflé at least two hours before baking. It is best when started at room temperature. Place baking dish in larger pan filled 1″ deep with water. Bake in preheated 350° F. oven for 1 hour. To test for doneness, insert knife into center. If it comes out clean, it is ready to serve.

Serves 4

2	Tablespoons butter
4	slices day-old bread
½	pound sharp cheddar cheese, grated
6	ounces dried beef
4	eggs
1½	cups milk
◆	Pinch of dry mustard
½	teaspoon salt
½	teaspoon pepper

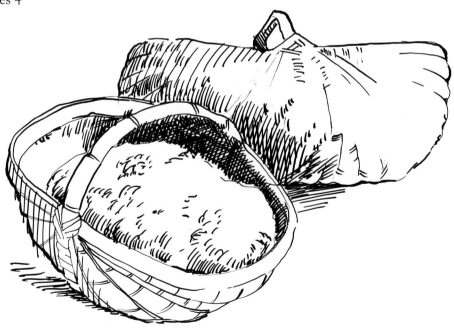

HELEN KEENE'S BAKED PINEAPPLE SOUFFLÉ

Helen and Ed have been good neighbors and friends as well as good cooks.

Beat eggs, flour and sugar thoroughly. Add pineapple and bread. Melt butter and add to above. Pour into 8" square baking dish and bake in a preheated 350° F. oven for 1 hour.

Excellent with baked ham.

Serves 6

- 3 **eggs**
- 2 **Tablespoons flour**
- ½ **cup sugar, less if desired**
- 20 **ounces (#2) canned crushed pineapple**
- 4 **slices white bread, cubed**
- ½ **cup butter or margarine**

CREAMED EGGS

For unusual serving, use Stoltzfus Pastry Squares, toast points or English muffins.

Place bread in buttered muffin cups to form patty shells. Bake in 350° F. oven until golden, approximately 6 minutes. Meanwhile, brown ham in butter in heavy sauce pan. Add onion and cook until soft. Stir in flour and gradually add milk. Cook until thick and smooth. Add sliced eggs and pour into toast cups or over toast.

Serves 6

- 6 **slices brown or white bread**
- 1½ **cups cooked or baked ham cut in strips or squares; bacon may be used**
- 3 **Tablespoons butter or margarine**
- ⅓ **cup chopped green onion**
- 3 **Tablespoons flour**
- 3 **cups milk**
- 6 **eggs, hard boiled, peeled and sliced**

EGG NOODLES

Fresh noodles are so much tastier than dried ones; it's like enjoying freshly-picked corn on the cob instead of frozen.

Place 2 cups of flour and the salt in a large mixing bowl. Make a well in the center and add the egg yolks and water. Stir until well blended. A food processor does this very quickly. Mix until you can work the dough into a ball, kneading to make it smooth. Cover with plastic wrap and let stand for at least 30 minutes. If using a pasta machine, cut dough according to directions. If rolling by hand, divide dough in thirds. Dust a generous amount of flour on top and bottom of each piece. Roll the dough as thin as you like the noodles, and flour both sides generously. Trim the edges, so that the dough is a neat square or rectangle. Starting at the one end, roll the dough into a very tight roll, as for a jelly roll. Using a sharp butcher knife, cut the roll into thin slices, approximately ¼" wide. As the slices fall onto the cutting board, toss them lightly with your hands so they do not stick together. Place on clean towels or a tablecloth to dry before cooking. Do not let them stick together. Noodles, after being thoroughly dried, may be stored in an airtight container for weeks. They also store well in the refrigerator or freezer. Cook as for Saffron Noodles.

2½ **cups all-purpose flour**
½ **teaspoon salt**
4 **egg yolks, or 3 whole eggs**
¼ **cup cold water**

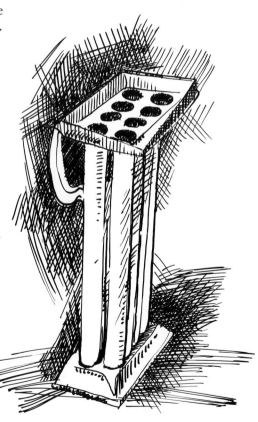

GREEN SPINACH NOODLES

For color, flavor and variation, serve these half and half with Egg Noodles.

Follow the same directions as for Egg Noodles, only add the spinach when mixing. Cook as for Saffron Noodles.

3 cups all-purpose flour
1 teaspoon salt
5 egg yolks
1 cup finely chopped fresh spinach or ½ cup thawed frozen spinach, drained
¼ cup cold water

SAFFRON NOODLES

Place salt, saffron, butter and water in a 2 quart sauce pan. Bring to a boil and add the noodles. Reduce heat to medium and boil, stirring occasionally, for approximately 10 minutes. Drain and serve with Browned Butter.

1½ teaspoons salt or salt substitute, ½ teaspoon pepper will substitute
◆ Pinch of saffron
1 Tablespoon butter or oil
1 quart water
3 cups noodles
Browned Butter or butter crumbs for topping (optional)

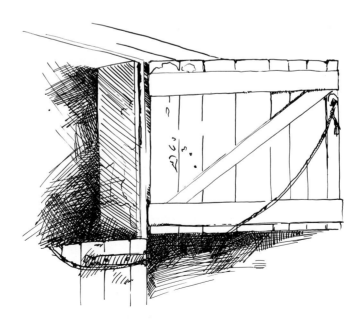

POT PIE SQUARES

Pennsylvania Dutch Pot Pie is not a baked pie, but a rich broth with noodle-type squares of dough boiled with the meat, thinly sliced potatoes, chopped celery and parsley. This one-dish meal has always been one of my favorites.

Follow Basic Noodle recipe, adding 1 Tablespoon butter or shortening.

RIVELS

These may be added to any rich stock to make a hearty soup. They are similar to German Spaetzle.

Break one egg into a one cup measure. Beat egg slightly and add enough milk to make the cup ¾ full. Pour into a mixing bowl and add salt and enough flour to make a dough you can crumble with your fingers. Rub the dough between your fingers in small crumbs, larger than cooked rice, and drop into rapidly boiling broth. Continue cooking for 3 minutes.

Rivels may be added to corn chowder, chicken corn soup, beef broth or any favorite stock.

1 egg
About ½ cup milk
½ teaspoon salt
About ¾ cup flour

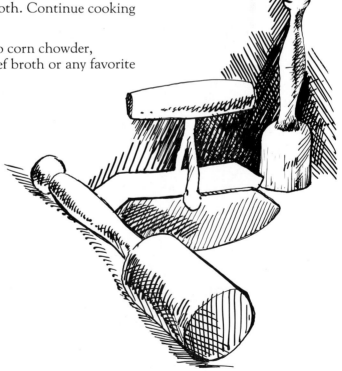

3

SOUPS & SIMMERS

SOUPS & SIMMERS

Just about everyone knows what chicken soup, "Jewish penicillin," can do for a cold. I'll bet you've never heard about the curative powers of brown flour potato soup.

According to my Mother and her friends, the soup could cure stomach ailments. I remember eating plenty of it when I was a child. But what I don't remember is ever eating it in the summer time. Apparently, either the brown flour potato soup's curative powers, or the ladies' will to make it, waned when the thermometer's mercury rose.

At any rate, the soup takes its name and gets its flavor from the curious practice of browning flour. To do it, measure the dry flour into a hot skillet and stir it constantly with a wooden spoon until it is a golden brown. Use the browned flour and butter to make a roux to thicken the soup and you'll find it has a rich, nutty flavor you won't find in any other potato soup.

The potato soup was quickly forgotten in mid summer when my Mother often made cold fruit soups for supper. No one ever complained because we all looked forward to these forerunners of today's more elaborate chilled soups.

Although the Cameron Estate Inn's blueberry soup and peach bisque (made with fresh peaches, cream, sour cream, brandy and nutmeg) are superb, my family's old-fashioned cold fruit soup isn't out-of-date, either. To create a taste of summer in a dish, simply toss fresh strawberries or raspberries with cubed homemade bread and sugar and pour fresh milk or cream over the mixture just before serving time.

In those days before people had embraced the lighter style of eating we know today, a midwinter meal of soup and little else was not greeted with nearly as much enthusiasm as were the cold soups of summer. When we sat down to such a supper, comments were liable to be "What did we do to deserve this?" or "Hasn't the milk check arrived yet?"

No soups ever stood alone, although they were practically thick enough to be stews and could be served on plates rather than in bowls. Fresh corn bread or hearty ham or beef brisket sandwiches prevented starvation during such "lean" times.

For a sampling of hearty old-fashioned soups we ate, try Flossie's country tomato herb soup, chicken corn chowder, cheddar cheese chowder, potato chowder and hamburger soup. Although I can't tell you what they'll do for stomach problems, I guarantee they're sure-fire cures for winter chills.

COCK AND BULL SOUP

A clear, mild flavored soup that's just right before a big meal.

Combine the chicken and beef broths and the water in a medium size saucepan. Peel the onion and press the cloves into it, then add it to the soup and bring it to a boil. Reduce the heat and simmer, covered, for 15 minutes. Remove the onion and stir in the brandy.

For added interest, float cheese-flavored croutons, popcorn or a very thin slice of lemon on top of the soup as it's being dished.

4 cups chicken broth, good, strong stock
2 cups beef broth, strong stock
2 to 3 cups of water, depending on how mild you want the soup
1 medium onion, whole
3 whole cloves
4 to 6 Tablespoons brandy

BASIC BEEF STOCK

The secret to an extra tasty stock is the roasting of the beef bones.

Place beef in a pan and roast in a pre-heated 400° F. oven for approximately 30 minutes until brown. Remove. Put the meat and bones in a stockpot with all the other ingredients. Bring to a boil. Reduce the heat to medium and simmer for at least an hour. Cool, skim the fat from the top and strain. Refrigerate, or freeze, for future use.

Makes 1 quart

HINT: To clarify the stock, whip 2 egg whites with dash of vinegar until frothy. Whip into the broth and slowly bring to a boil. When it reaches the boiling point, remove from heat and strain through double cheesecloth.

2 to 3 pounds beef bones with meat (rib bones, leftover beef roasts or rib roasts are superb)
6 cups water
1 Tablespoon salt (less if meat was seasoned)
½ teaspoon black pepper
1 bay leaf
1 Tablespoon chopped parsley
¼ cup chopped celery with leaves
1 teaspoon chopped thyme
¼ cup diced onion

HAMBURGER SOUP

Mary Anne Lutz shared this favorite with my cooking school students at the Hotel Hershey. It's great for a big party, is low in calories and freezes well. The longer it simmers, the better it tastes.

Brown the beef in a large, heavy stockpot. Drain off all fat. Add all the ingredients and bring to a boil. Simmer for 2 hours. Remove the bay leaf.

2 pounds ground beef
½ head of cabbage
46 ounces tomato juice
2 cups sliced carrots
1 pound can of stewed tomatoes, diced
2 cups chopped celery
6½ ounces canned minced clams including juice
2 teaspoons fresh basil
1 teaspoon fresh oregano
1 teaspoon salt or salt substitute
1 teaspoon coarsely ground pepper
3 Tablespoons minced onions
16 fresh mushrooms or 8 ounces, canned
1 bay leaf
1 Tablespoon worcestershire sauce
1 clove garlic, minced
2 pounds green beans, cut

BASIC CHICKEN STOCK

Place all ingredients in a stockpot and bring to a boil. Reduce heat to low and simmer for at least 1 hour. Strain through a cheesecloth. Cool. Refrigerate, or freeze for future use.

- 3 pounds chicken pieces, backs, wings, necks, etc., including hearts and gizzards. Do not use the livers
- 4 cups water
- ◆ Pinch of saffron
- 1½ teaspoons salt (more or less if desired)
- ½ teaspoon pepper
- ½ teaspoon thyme
- ◆ Pinch of tarragon
- 1 teaspoon chopped parsley
- ¼ cup chopped celery with leaves
- ½ cup grated carrots
- 1 Tablespoon diced celery root (optional)
- ¼ cup chopped onion (optional)

DAVE'S CREAM OF CHICKEN SOUP

In large stockpot, simmer the stock, celery, onion, parsley, chicken, basil and thyme for approximately 30 minutes. In saucepan, melt butter and stir in the flour until smooth. Slowly add milk or cream and stir until thickened. Gradually add the milk or cream mixture to chicken stock and check for taste. Add salt and pepper if desired.

NOTE: This may be used as a substitute for canned cream of chicken soup.

- 5 cups chicken stock
- ½ cup chopped celery
- ¾ cup chopped onion
- 2 Tablespoons chopped parsley
- 1 cup finely diced cooked chicken
- 1 teaspoon fresh basil, ½ if dried
- 1 teaspoon fresh thyme, ½ if dried
- 3 Tablespoons butter
- 5 Tablespoons flour
- 1 cup milk or cream
- Salt and white pepper to taste

CHICKEN CORN CHOWDER

An interesting version of chicken corn soup.

Rinse chicken and pat dry. Melt butter in a large stockpot and brown the whole chicken. Add 1½ quarts water, broth, celery, onion, salt, pepper and saffron. Bring to a boil, then simmer, covered, for an hour until chicken is tender. Remove the chicken and add the corn and the noodles and cook until the noodles are soft. Remove the meat from the bones, cut into pieces and return to the pot. Add the eggs and parsley and more salt and pepper if desired.

Makes more than 3 quarts

1 (3 pound) roasting chicken
2 Tablespoons butter or margarine
4 cups undiluted chicken broth
1 large onion, peeled and quartered
3 ribs of celery, including leaves
2½ teaspoons salt
¾ teaspoon pepper
¼ teaspoon saffron
8 ounce package noodles, medium width
1½ cups frozen corn
3 hard boiled eggs, chopped coarsely
2 Tablespoons fresh parsley, chopped

OYSTER STEW

Put oysters in colander and drain the liquid into large saucepan. Check each oyster for shells, gently pressing them with your fingers, being careful not to break them. Heat the oyster liquid and add butter and seasonings. When nearly boiling, add the milk and cream. Add the oysters and remove from heat. Serve in heated bowls with oyster crackers or your favorite breads. Sprinkle a dash of paprika in center of each bowl.

2 dozen oysters with liquid
3 Tablespoons butter
½ teaspoon celery seed
½ teaspoon seafood seasoning
3 cups milk
1 cup light cream
Paprika
1 teaspoon salt (optional)

BASIC CREAM OF MUSHROOM SOUP

This may be used in any recipe calling for cream of mushroom soup.

Place mushrooms, stock, onion, celery and basil in large stockpot. Bring to a boil and simmer 30 minutes. In saucepan melt the butter and stir in the flour, stirring until smooth. Remove a cup of the stock mixture and slowly add to the flour until thickened. Pour back into stockpot and add cream or milk. Check for seasonings, adding salt and pepper if desired. Heat, but do not boil.

For serving as a soup, you may add more milk or stock if desired.

2 pounds mushrooms, chopped
1 quart chicken stock
½ cup diced onion
1 cup finely chopped celery
1 Tablespoon fresh basil
3 Tablespoons butter
5 Tablespoons flour
1 cup cream (milk if desired)

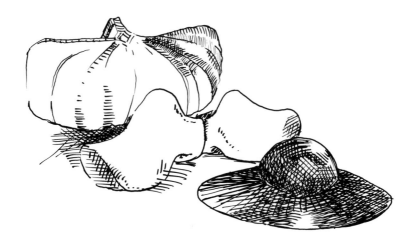

CHEDDAR CHEESE CHOWDER

In heavy stockpot, simmer the stock, onion, celery, herbs and carrots for at least 30 minutes. Melt butter in saucepan and stir in flour until smooth. Add one cup of the stock and stir until thickened. Add thickened mixture to above and add cheeses, stirring until dissolved. Add the cream or milk and heat to near boiling. Garnish with croutons or popped corn.

Serves 6 to 8

- 1 quart chicken stock
- ½ cup diced onion
- ½ cup diced celery
- ½ teaspoon chopped basil
- ½ teaspoon chives or oregano
- 1 cup grated carrots
- 2 Tablespoons butter
- 3 Tablespoons flour
- ¾ pound sharp cheddar cheese, grated
- ½ pound port wine cheese
- 1 cup heavy cream (for lighter fare, use milk)

Pepper to taste

FLOSSIE'S OLD FASHIONED TOMATO SOUP

This is one of the favorite soups served at our Cameron Estate Inn.

In heavy stockpot, simmer the broth, tomatoes, sugar, herbs, and seasonings for 30 minutes. In saucepan, melt the butter and stir in the flour until smooth. Gradually add the milk or cream, stirring until thickened. Pour into stockpot and stir until thoroughly heated but not boiling. Garnish. Fresh basil leaf or watercress looks and tastes great.

- 1 quart rich chicken broth
- 1 gallon peeled, diced tomatoes with juice
- 1 cup sugar (less if desired)
- 1 teaspoon chopped parsley
- 1 teaspoon chopped basil

Salt and pepper to taste

- 3 Tablespoons butter
- 5 Tablespoons flour
- 1 quart half-and-half, milk, or half milk and half evaporated milk

POTATO SOUP

Place potatoes, stock, herbs, celery, onion and carrots in a large stockpot. Bring to boil and simmer for 30 minutes. Remove bay leaf. In a saucepan, melt the butter and stir in the flour until smooth. Use 1 cup of the above liquid and stir into flour mixture until thickened. Pour into potato soup and stir until thoroughly heated. Add salt or pepper if desired. The sliced eggs may be added to the soup before serving or used on top as garnish. Garnish with parsley.

3 cups diced potatoes
4 cups chicken stock
1 teaspoon thyme
1 teaspoon basil
1 bay leaf
½ cup chopped celery
½ cup chopped onion
½ cup grated carrots
2 Tablespoons butter
3 Tablespoons flour
2 hard boiled eggs, peeled and sliced
Salt and pepper to taste
Parsley to garnish

BROWN FLOUR POTATO SOUP

You'll love this variation, I'm sure.

Cook the potatoes, celery and onions in 2 cups of water for 10 minutes. Place the flour in a heavy skillet on medium heat. Stir constantly with a wooden spoon or spatula until flour turns medium brown, not burnt, approximately 10 minutes. Add the butter and stir until smooth. Remove from heat and gradually add milk, stirring with a wire whisk. Place on medium heat and stir until thoroughly heated. Add cooked potatoes, celery, onions, celery seed, salt and pepper. Garnish with a sprig of parsley.

- 3 cups diced potatoes
- ½ cup diced onion
- ½ cup chopped celery
- 2 eggs, hard boiled
- ½ teaspoon celery seed
- 1 teaspoon salt
- ½ teaspoon coarsely ground pepper
- ⅓ cup butter or margarine
- ½ cup flour
- 4 cups milk

Few sprigs of parsley

CHILLED PEACH BISQUE

A guest at our Cameron Estate Inn said this was so delicious she would like to use it as a facial.

Puree the peaches with sugar in blender or food processor. Add sour cream, half-and-half and cream. Refrigerate and allow to sit for several hours to draw the flavors. Add brandy (optional) just before serving. Sprinkle top of each serving with cinnamon. Top with a dollop of whipped cream or a slice of fresh peach.

Placing the soup bowls in the freezer before serving will keep the soup cold for a longer period of time.

1 **pound fresh or frozen drained peaches, peeled**
6 **Tablespoons brown sugar**
8 **ounces sour cream**
1 **quart half-and-half (milk may be used for a lighter soup)**
1 **pint heavy whipping cream**
⅛ **cup brandy**
2 **Tablespoons cinnamon**
Whipped cream or fresh peach slices for garnish

BLUEBERRY SOUP

Chilled, this is a perfectly beautiful, refreshing summer soup.

Soften gelatin in cold water. Stir until dissolved. In large saucepan combine cran-blueberry juice, lemon juice, sugar and blueberries. Bring to boil and simmer 15 minutes. Remove from heat and strain. Add the gelatin mixture and mix thoroughly. Chill until soup is slightly thick. Pour into chilled bowls and serve with a dollop of sour cream and a few blueberries.

Serves 6 to 8

2 packages (1 Tablespoon each) unflavored gelatin
½ cup cold water
4 cups cran-blueberry or orange juice (cran-apple may be used)
3 Tablespoons lemon juice
¼ cup sugar
2 cups fresh blueberries
Sour cream and fresh berries for topping

CHIPPED BEEF CASSEROLE

Blend the soup and milk together, then add the cooked potatoes, onion, pepper, cheese, and the beef. Spoon into a buttered casserole and top with chips and the butter. Bake in a preheated 350° F. oven for 20 to 30 minutes until bubbly and browned.

1½ cups cream of chicken soup
¾ cup milk
3 cups cooked potatoes, diced
3 Tablespoons finely chopped onion
¼ teaspoon coarse pepper
1 cup cheddar cheese, grated
1½ cups chipped beef, shredded
2 Tablespoons butter, melted
1 cup potato chips, crushed

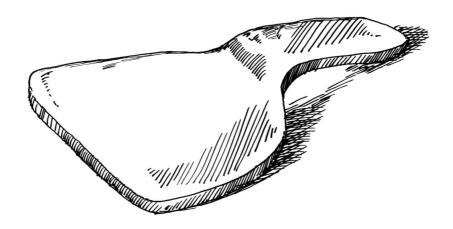

JARLSBERG VEGETABLE BAKE

Sauté eggplant in the oil until lightly browned and set aside. Cook the zucchini, mushrooms, green pepper and onion for several minutes and add tomatoes, salt and pepper. Alternate layers of vegetables and cheese in a shallow 1½ quart buttered baking dish. Top with cheese and bake in a preheated 350° F. oven for 30 minutes.

1 medium eggplant, peeled and sliced
¼ cup oil
3 medium zucchini, sliced
1 cup mushrooms, sliced
½ cup green pepper, cut in strips
½ cup onion, chopped
1 cup cherry tomatoes, halved
1 teaspoon salt
¼ teaspoon pepper
2 cups Jarlsberg cheese, shredded

BAKED HASH

A MICROWAVE is the time-saver in this recipe.

If you have a MICROWAVE, cook the diced potatoes in 4 Tablespoons of water for about 10 minutes, then drain. While they're cooking, brown the onion in the butter, then brown the beef cubes. Add the salt and pepper, worcestershire and parsley and toss lightly with the drained potatoes. Place in a medium sized casserole, properly greased, and pour the broth over the contents. Bake in a preheated 350° F. oven, uncovered, for 45 minutes to an hour until the top is browned but not dried out. If the meat looks like it's getting too dry, cover during the last part of the cooking time.

4 cups diced potatoes
2 cups, 1 pound beef cubes
1 Tablespoon butter
1 Tablespoon chopped onion (more if desired)
⅛ teaspoon pepper
2 teaspoons worcestershire sauce
2 teaspoons chopped parsley
1 cup beef broth or bouillon
1 teaspoon salt (optional)

SOUPER MEAT 'N POTATO PIE

Mix thoroughly ½ cup of the soup, beef, onion, egg, bread crumbs, parsley and seasonings. Firmly press the mixture into a 9″ pie plate, forming a shell and bake in a preheated 350° F. oven for 25 minutes. Spoon off any fat. Frost with the mashed potatoes and top with remaining soup and cheese. Return to the oven and bake for another 10 minutes. Garnish with the cooked bacon. Allow it to stand at least 5 minutes before cutting.

1½ cups cream of mushroom soup
1 pound ground chuck, beef
¼ cup onion, finely chopped
1 egg, slightly beaten
¼ cup fine, dry bread crumbs
2 Tablespoons chopped parsley
¼ teaspoon salt
◆ Dash pepper
2 cups mashed potatoes
¼ cup mild cheddar, shredded
4 slices bacon, cooked

SAUSAGE AND SWEET POTATOES

An attractive, tasty "company" casserole.

Peel and slice the potatoes ½" thick and cook in salted water until almost soft. Cook the sausage until browned and pour off any excess fat. Arrange the potatoes in a greased casserole in two layers. Mix water and lemon juice together and add two of the apples which have been peeled and sliced ¼" thick. The third apple should only be cored, not peeled, and cut into 8 slices then added to the liquid. The juice prevents the apples from turning brown. Cover the potato layer with a layer of peeled apple slices, then pour the remaining liquid over all. Top the two layers with the sausage and spoon the applesauce over that in the center of the baking dish, leaving the outside two inches of the dish uncovered. Sprinkle the sauce with the cinnamon and crumble the brown sugar on top. Arrange the remaining apple over the applesauce, peel side up, like the spokes on a wheel. Bake in a preheated 375° F. oven for 30 to 40 minutes. If desired, halfway through the baking time, add prunes that have been soaked in water or rubbed with cooking oil. Put a prune between each apple slice for added interest.

MICROWAVE: Cover with waxed paper and bake 15 to 18 minutes.

  6 sweet potatoes or yams
  1 teaspoon salt
1½ pounds loose pork sausage
  3 tart green apples
1½ Tablespoons lemon juice
  ¼ cup water
  ⅓ cup brown sugar, packed
  1 cup applesauce, unsweetened
  ½ teaspoon cinnamon
 10 dried prunes (optional)

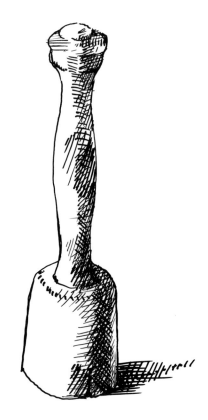

GOULASH

Brown meat in oil with salt and pepper. Remove meat to a platter, add the onion and sesame seeds to the drippings and brown lightly. Stir in the paprika, dry mustard, bay leaf, worcestershire, wine, tomatoes and water. Cook for 5 minutes. Return meat to the saucepan, cover and simmer on low heat for 1½ hours until meat is tender. If the goulash seems too thick add another splash of wine or water until the mixture is the desired consistency. Add the olives last and heat thoroughly. Garnish with parsley and serve on noodles with sour cream for topping.

Serves 8

2 pounds boneless beef chuck, 1″ cubes
2 Tablespoons vegetable oil
1 teaspoon salt
¼ teaspoon coarsely ground pepper
1 medium onion, chopped
3 Tablespoons sesame seeds
1 teaspoon sweet paprika
1 teaspoon dry mustard
1 bay leaf
1 Tablespoon worcestershire sauce
½ cup dry red wine
1 pound stewed tomatoes
1 Tablespoon brown sugar
1 cup water
1 7 ounce can pitted ripe olives, drained and cut in half
2 Tablespoons parsley, chopped

TIPSY DOGS

This is a recipe for entertaining a party of 25 or more, but is easily cut down to fit your family's needs. The dogs are great served whole in a crusty roll.

In a crockpot or saucepan, combine the catsup, brown sugar, mustard, horseradish and bourbon. Cut the hot dogs in bite size, 1″ pieces or leave them whole and simmer them in the sauce for 3 to 4 hours on low heat.

5 pounds hot dogs
3 cups catsup
1 cup brown sugar
1 cup mustard
2 Tablespoons horseradish
½ cup bourbon

CHILI

Brown hamburg in skillet and drain off fat. Transfer the meat to a large saucepan or crockpot. Melt butter in skillet and lightly brown the onions. Add them to the meat along with the salt and pepper, tomatoes, beans, and tabasco and simmer for 1 to 2 hours. The longer it cooks the better it gets. Some people like it even better reheated a day or so later.

1 pound lean ground beef or chuck
1 Tablespoon butter or margarine
1 teaspoon salt
2/3 cup onion, chopped
1/2 cup green pepper, chopped
3 cups diced tomatoes in sauce
2 Tablespoons brown sugar
2 cups canned kidney beans
2 cups great northern beans
◆ Dash of tabasco
Grated cheddar cheese and chopped onion for topping

SCALLOPED HAM AND VEGETABLES

The MICROWAVE is the time-saver again in this recipe. All of the vegetables are precooked and the MICROWAVE keeps them from being overdone and mushy and cuts down the baking time. The color combination of the foods make it an attractive buffet dish.

Grease a 3 quart casserole or 9" x 13" baking dish. Cook the sliced potatoes in the MICROWAVE, covered with wax paper, in 1" of water for 15 minutes. Drain and place in the casserole. Cook the carrots and broccoli the same way for 7 minutes each and add the ham cubes and drained vegetables to the potatoes. In a skillet, melt the butter and lightly brown the onions. Stir in the flour and gradually add the milk, stirring constantly until smooth and thickened. Season with salt and pepper and pour over the layered ingredients. Top with grated cheese and drizzle with butter if desired. Bake in a preheated 400° F. oven for 30 minutes or until bubbling and lightly golden.

Serves 8 to 10

3 cups cooked ham, cut into 1" cubes
4 to 5 cups sliced cooked potatoes, approximately 7 medium
2 cups sliced cooked carrots
2 cups cooked broccoli buds
3 Tablespoons butter or margarine
Medium onion, chopped
1/3 cup flour
3 cups milk
1 teaspoon salt
Coarsely ground pepper to taste
3/4 to 1 cup cheddar cheese, grated
2 Tablespoons butter, melted (optional)

4

FISH & SEAFOOD

FISH & SEAFOOD

Simon Cameron, Abraham Lincoln's infamous Secretary of War and the man who lived in our Cameron Estate Inn, was a brilliant capitalist and one of the most skilled political manipulators in America during his time.

His tactics that always added to his personal fortunes, often at the expense of the Union, once led Lincoln to ask politician Thaddeus Stevens of Lancaster, "You don't think Mr. Cameron would steal, do you?" Stevens answered, "Well, he wouldn't steal a red hot stove."

Needless to say, with his pockets well-lined, Cameron knew how to live well. According to reports, when he was living in the house, he arose at 8 A.M. to have toast, a chop and a few soft-boiled eggs. At 11 A.M. he had champagne which he claimed added 50 years to his life. In the evening he often dined on roast beef and baked apples but stayed away from pies because he believed pie eaters would die young. Before retiring, he had a few glasses of rye in the library.

But Simon did use a portion of his fortune to do us all a favor. While on a trip to his native Scotland, he decided to import trout and knowledgeable fish tenders to care for them. When he returned home with his live cargo, he established a hatchery at Donegal Springs, which begins at the Inn.

We figure the pecan-flavored trout, an Inn specialty in which the fish is dredged in corn meal and crushed pecans, would have appealed to the health-minded Simon.

In his memory, we also keep the stream that meanders through the Inn property and the Farm's pond well-stocked with trout. Our guests who have fishing tackle are welcome to try catching their own dinners. Anyone who's particularly hungry would be smart to fish at the farm because the fish at the Inn are as cunning as the man who brought their ancestors to Lancaster County.

Although I've included a number of other seafood specialties from the Inn and the Farm, from crepes and clam fritters to deviled clams, shad roe with bacon and my son Charlie's fried oysters, there's no dish I like more than simple pan-fried trout.

If you're pan frying trout at home, give my way a try. I don't remove the fins or the head until the fish is cooked. At that point, a fork inserted under the back bone will be all that's needed to neatly fillet the fish in a matter of seconds and make you look like a culinary pro.

DUCHESS FLORENTINE BAKED FISH

No one will know how easy this dish is to prepare, and it is guaranteed to impress your guests.

Place fillets in a buttered baking dish and sprinkle with lemon juice. Beat one egg lightly and mix with spinach, nutmeg, dry mustard, salt, pepper and chervil. Spoon mixture over fish. Beat the other egg with the prepared potatoes. If the potatoes are too stiff, add a bit of milk, since you want to spread or pipe them (with pastry bag and large star tip) over the above mixture. Top with paprika and bake in a preheated 375° F. oven for 25 to 30 minutes, checking the fish for flaking, or until lightly browned. Garnish with lemon slices and capers.

NOTE: If using frozen fish and frozen spinach, drain spinach thoroughly and thaw fish in microwave for 20 minutes. Use 1 extra egg and ½ cup of bread crumbs with spinach mixture.

1 **pound fresh fish fillets**
1 **Tablespoon lemon juice**
2 **eggs**
3 **cups fresh spinach, chopped**
¼ **teaspoon nutmeg**
¼ **teaspoon dry mustard**
½ **teaspoon salt**
½ **teaspoon pepper**
1 **teaspoon chervil (parsley may be substituted)**
3 **cups mashed potatoes, seasoned**
Paprika
Lemon slices and capers for garnish

HADDOCK WITH VEGETABLES OR "SUPPER IN A SACK"

This MICROWAVE dish is the working woman's favorite. By doubling the recipe and using a large broasting bag, the size for a turkey, it's pretty enough to serve at your next dinner party. Place the bag on a large platter and cut it open just before serving, or even at the table.

Rinse fish and pat dry with paper towels. Place in broaster bag. Slice all the vegetables and arrange on top of fish. Mix wine, salt and pepper and pour over the vegetables. The bag will be very full. Tighten top with plastic tie and place in shallow MICRO-WAVE baking dish. Cut six ½" slits in the top of the bag with a sharp knife. Cook on high for approximately 15 minutes or until vegetables are crunchy. Do not overcook. Drain most of the broth and pour into a small pitcher or gravy boat. Place the dinner on a beautiful platter and fold the bag decoratively, garnishing with fresh parsley. Serve with hearty, crusty bread for dipping.

1 to 1½ pounds haddock fillets
1 medium zucchini, sliced
1 medium yellow squash, sliced
3 ¼" thick slices onion, separated into rings
2 tomatoes, thickly sliced
8 to 10 medium sized mushrooms, quartered
1 bunch fresh parsley, keep part for garnish
1 cup white wine
1 teaspoon salt
½ teaspoon coarse pepper

TROUT — CAMERON ESTATE STYLE

The infamous Simon Cameron brought trout to Pennsylvania, starting a fish hatchery here at his summer mansion, which is now our Cameron Estate Inn.

You may want to use trout that are boned and beheaded, but if you are catching your own, give my way a try. Don't remove the fins or the head until the fish is cooked. At that point, a fork inserted under the back bone will be all that's needed to neatly fillet the fish in a matter of seconds. Dredge the trout in flour, then dip in egg wash. Bread each trout in pecan breading. Melt butter or oil in large sauté pan and place trout skin side up. Season lightly with pepper and salt if desired. Sauté until edges start to curl, then flip over and cook until the fish flakes with fork when inserted at thickest part. Gently remove fish onto heated platter. Add wine and lemon juice to brownings. Deglaze pan and pour sauce over the fish. Garnish with capers, lemon slices and watercress.

VARIATION

This recipe may be used for any fresh, whole fish. Chopped green scallions may be added when deglazing pan for variation in sauce.

1 trout per person
Flour for dredging
Egg wash (beaten egg with 1 teaspoon water)
Pecan breading
White pepper
Butter or oil for frying
⅓ cup white wine
1 Tablespoon lemon juice
Capers, lemon slices and watercress for garnish
Salt (optional); the breading substitutes for salt

CHIP BREADED FLOUNDER

Here's a good way to use up those last potato chips in the bag. Choose one of the many different flavored chips on the market today for breading your fish.

Rinse the fillets and pat them dry with paper towels. Mix the salt and pepper with the flour and coat the fish. Dip into the beaten egg and then coat with a layer of the chips, making sure the breading is patted on firmly with your hands. If time allows, let stand in the refrigerator for about a half hour before pan frying so the coating will stick better. Put the oil in a large skillet over medium heat and brown the fillets on both sides. When they are browned, turn the heat down, add the butter and continue cooking for a total of 7 to 8 minutes on each side. Don't overcook.

6 flounder fillets
Salt and freshly ground pepper to taste
½ cup flour for dredging
2 eggs, lightly beaten with 1 Tablespoon water
1½ cups sour cream potato chips, finely crushed
4 Tablespoons vegetable oil
3 to 4 Tablespoons butter
Fresh parsley
½ lemon, thinly sliced

PECAN BREADING

This is an excellent breading if you want to avoid salt. Great for chicken, too. Make this ahead and keep in refrigerator.

Place all ingredients in food processor or blender and blend thoroughly. Store in refrigerator or freezer for use as you need it.

1 cup bread crumbs
1 cup corn meal
1 cup pecans, finely crushed

PAN FRIED PERCH

Clean the fish, removing the eyes. Lightly salt the inside of each fish. Place flour, salt, seafood seasoning, and pepper in a plastic bag. Shake each fish in the flour mixture.

Heat the butter in a large heavy skillet. Add fish, frying until golden brown, approximately 6 minutes on each side. Place whole fish on heated platter. Put fresh parsley in eye sockets of fish. Arrange a slice or two of lemon on each fish. To fillet, gently lift up the head of the fish. Place a fork behind the gill and center backbone. Pull the head back towards the tail. The whole backbone will come away from the fish, leaving the bottom fillet on the platter. Turn the fish. The spine with all the bones intact will lift out easily.

6   fresh perch
¾   cup flour
¾   teaspoon salt
¾   teaspoon seafood seasoning
◆   Dash pepper
6   Tablespoons butter
Lemon wedges
Parsley

SWEET AND SOUR SEAFOOD KABOBS

Marinate overnight in refrigerator for easy entertaining the next day.

Place seafood and vegetables on skewers in any order desired, alternating fish and vegetables. Place kabobs in marinade for several hours or overnight. Lightly season with salt and pepper if desired. Place on hot grill or bake in 375° F. oven until seafood turns white, approximately 10 to 15 minutes. Serve on a bed of rice or pasta.

Serves 4

MARINADE

1½   cups brown sugar
1   Tablespoon prepared hot mustard
⅓   cup lemon juice
1   clove garlic, crushed

KABOBS

½   pound shrimp, peeled and deveined
½   pound scallops
½   pound any firm fresh fish (salmon, sword, tuna, snapper, etc.)
2   green or red bell peppers, cubed
1   pint mushrooms, cleaned
1   pint cherry tomatoes
Rice or pasta of your choice

SCALLOPED OYSTERS

This has always been a "special" dish we served with roast turkey or prime rib.

Arrange a layer of crackers in a shallow, buttered baking dish. Place half of the oysters on the crumbs and wet with the oyster liquid. Sprinkle with the lemon juice, pepper and half of the butter, then do another layer of crackers and oysters. Beat egg with the milk and pour over the casserole. Top with bread cubes or crumbs and drizzle with the rest of the butter. Bake in a preheated 400° F. oven for 30 to 40 minutes, or until bubbly and golden brown.

2 cups oysters, freshly shucked, or 2 cans, 8 ounces each
2 cups crackers, slightly crushed
¾ cup oyster liquid, drained from cans
1 Tablespoon lemon juice
4 Tablespoons butter, melted
¼ teaspoon coarse pepper
1 large egg
¾ cup half-and-half or milk
½ cup buttered bread cubes or crumbs
Paprika

CHARLIE'S FRIED OYSTERS

The secret for the extra flavor is the dry mustard.

Drain the liquid from the oysters, reserving ¼ cup to mix with the egg. Check each oyster for shells. Pat the oysters dry and roll in a mixture of crumbs, dry mustard, salt and pepper. Dip them in the egg and oyster liquid and roll in crumbs again. The breading sticks to the oyster better if they are chilled for at least 30 minutes before frying. Pan fry or deep fry until golden brown, not more than 5 minutes.

24 large oysters
¼ cup oyster liquid
½ cup fresh bread crumbs
½ cup crushed cracker crumbs
½ teaspoon dry mustard
½ teaspoon pepper
1 egg, lightly beaten

GOLDEN BATTER DIPPED SHRIMP

Peel and devein shrimp. Dredge in flour. Heat shortening to 375° F. Dip in beer batter. Drop several pieces at a time in heated shortening, either by deep frying or pan frying. Fry until golden brown. Drain on paper towels. Keep warm until serving.

1½ **pounds shrimp, peeled**
Flour for dredging
Beer batter for coating
Shortening for frying

VARIATION

Batter dipped fish may be substituted by using 1½ pounds fresh or frozen fish. Check fish and remove any small bones. Pat dry, then follow instructions above.

BEER BATTER

This batter can be used for vegetables or fish.

Mix all the batter ingredients in a blender or mixer. Chill and cover for at least 30 minutes. It is better if it is refrigerated overnight.

1½ **cups all-purpose flour**
 ½ **teaspoon salt**
  1 **Tablespoon baking powder**
 ½ **teaspoon white pepper**
 ¼ **cup milk**
  1 **cup beer**
  1 **egg**

SHRIMP AND SCALLOPS ROMANOFF

Melt butter in large skillet. Dredge shrimp in flour and place in skillet, adding scallops, pepper, garlic and salt. When nearly cooked, add the wine and lemon juice. Simmer for 1 minute and add cream, beaten egg and shredded cheese. When thickened and completely heated, pour over hot linguini. Serve with dollop of sour cream and dot center with caviar or olive.

1 pound shrimp, peeled and deveined
1 pound scallops
¼ cup butter
Flour for dredging
½ teaspoon white pepper
Clove of garlic, crushed
Salt, if desired
½ cup white wine
1 Tablespoon lemon juice
1 cup cream
1 egg, lightly beaten
½ cup parmesan cheese, shredded
½ pound linguini, cooked and seasoned
¼ cup sour cream
1 Tablespoon caviar; black olive could be substituted

CAJUN SHRIMP

Our Bayou friends gave me their favorite summer grill recipe. It is out of this world. Served with French bread, it is a perfect meal.

Place shrimp in the center of a 24" strip of heavy aluminum foil. Sprinkle with the pepper, lemon slices, and dots of butter. Pour the dressing over everything. Wrap foil tightly to seal and place on hot grill or a 450° F. oven for 20 minutes. If baking in oven, place in baking pan. Remove from heat and serve on large heated platter, folding back the foil to form bowl. Use broth for dipping of bread. Everyone enjoys shelling their own shrimp.

The shells of the shrimp keep the meat from being too "hot," but you can vary the pepper as you like.

Serves 6 to 8

3 pounds large shrimp in shells
1 cup Italian salad dressing
3 Tablespoons coarsely ground black pepper
½ cup butter (1 stick)
1 lemon, thinly sliced
Loaf of French or Hearty bread

CLAM FRITTERS

This seashore staple is always available with canned clams from your pantry shelf.

Drain clams and reserve juice. Sift the flour, baking powder, salt, and pepper together. Mix the juice and eggs, and add the clams. Combine both mixtures and stir until well blended. Drop by tablespoonsful into hot oil in a skillet. Cook until golden brown on both sides and drain on paper towels.

Makes 10–12 fritters

2 6½ ounce cans minced clams
1⅓ cups all-purpose flour, sifted
2 teaspoons baking powder
⅛ teaspoon pepper
½ cup clam juice, drained from cans
2 eggs, slightly beaten
Oil for frying
¾ teaspoon salt (optional)

DEVILED CLAMS

Chop the clams into small pieces. Put the eggs, onion, celery, and pepper into a blender and chop very fine. Add the clams, the egg mixture, parsley and bread crumbs until well blended. Season to taste with salt and pepper. Scrub 20 clam shells and butter the inside. Fry the clams upside down in hot butter until golden brown or bake in a preheated 375° F. oven for 25 minutes.

Allow 2 clams per person

10 large clams
4 eggs, lightly beaten
½ medium onion
2 large ribs celery
½ large green pepper
2 Tablespoons chopped parsley
4 cups fresh bread crumbs
Salt and freshly ground pepper
1 Tablespoon butter

LOBSTER MICHAEL

Repeat customers at our Cameron Estate Inn request it. You'll love it!

Remove the lobster from the shell and butterfly by cutting ⅔ through center of meat from end to end. Dip in egg wash then dredge in flour. Melt butter in skillet or sauté pan and add lobster tails. Season and sauté until golden brown. Turn and season with rest of seasonings and brown lightly. Add enough wine to nearly cover the lobster. Cover with lid and reduce wine until only a nice sauce is left (about ¼ liquid). Sprinkle with lemon juice and serve over buttered pasta. Garnish with parsley.

VARIATION

Large shrimp are great as a substitute.

1 lobster tail, raw, for each person
4 Tablespoons butter
Egg wash (egg beaten with 1 teaspoon milk)
Flour for dredging
◆ Dash of salt, pepper, garlic salt for each
◆ Pinch of ground sage for each
◆ Pinch of chopped parsley for each
Wine
Lemon juice
Parsley for garnish
Pasta of your choice

SHAD ROE WITH BACON

Roe is best when served with new potatoes and garden peas.

Wash the roe carefully so as not to break the thin membrane. Drain well and dust with a thin coating of flour. Season each with salt and pepper. Sauté the roe gently in bacon fat until golden brown. Cook at a medium temperature to keep the membranes from breaking and scattering the roe. Carefully turn and sauté the other side. Remove to a heated platter and garnish with crisp bacon and a lemon wedge.

Serves 8

4 **pairs of shad roe**
¼ **cup flour**
Salt and pepper
½ **pound bacon, fried crisp**
  Save fat for sautéeing roe
1 **lemon, cut into wedges**

SAUTÉED SCALLOPS WITH WINE GLAZE

Rinse scallops and pat dry, then coat lightly with flour. Melt the butter and sauté, turning often with a spoon. If they cook too long, the tender scallops will get tough — 10 minutes is plenty. Spoon over a bed of cooked rice on a platter, then deglaze the pan with the wine and pour the liquid over all. Top with a dash of paprika and garnish with lemon wedges.

1½ **pounds bay scallops or sea scallops, cut in quarters**
2 **Tablespoons butter**
¼ **cup flour**
⅛ **teaspoon white pepper**
½ **cup white wine**
Paprika
Lemon wedges

SEAFOOD CREPES

Making the crepes ahead of time is the secret to this elegant dish. The filling can be any combination of your favorite seafood.

Sauté the seafood in butter in a large heavy saucepan for approximately 10 minutes. Add the wine, lemon juice and seasonings and check for salt, adding a dash if desired. Simmer for 10 minutes. Add the white sauce and heat thoroughly.

Spoon the mixture into the center of each crepe and overlap both sides. Place seam side down on heated serving platter. Top with sauce.

- 3 cups thick white sauce
- ½ cup butter
- 1 cup bay scallops
- 1 cup shrimp, peeled and deveined
- 1 cup crab meat
- ½ cup lobster (optional)
- 1 cup sliced mushrooms
- ¼ cup green and red peppers, chopped
- ¼ cup onion, chopped
- ½ cup canned artichoke hearts, chopped
- ¼ cup white wine
- 2 Tablespoons lemon juice
- ½ teaspoon white pepper
- ◆ Dash of Old Bay seasoning
- ◆ Dash of paprika

Sauce for top — see recipe below

DAVE'S SAUCE FOR SEAFOOD CREPES

The boiling butter, not browned, thickens the sauce as it is poured into the egg mixture, thus making it an easy Hollandaise sauce.

Combine all ingredients but the butter in food processor or mixer and blend thoroughly. Bring butter to a boil and slowly pour butter into above mixture while mixing on high speed until thickened. Can be kept warm, but do not bring to a boil or sauce will break.

- 2 eggs
- ½ teaspoon tabasco
- 1 Tablespoon lemon juice
- 1 chicken bouillon cube
- ½ teaspoon paprika
- ½ pound butter, boiling

SEAFOOD AMARETTO

Melt butter in heavy saucepan or skillet. Dredge shrimp in flour and place in skillet. Add scallops, crab meat and seasonings. Let cook for a few minutes, or until the scallops turn white. Add lemon juice, Amaretto and heavy cream. Heat thoroughly and serve over bed of steaming rice.

½ pound shrimp, peeled and deveined
½ pound sea scallops
½ cup crab meat
4 Tablespoons butter
Flour for dredging
½ teaspoon white pepper
1 teaspoon parsley, chopped
1 teaspoon lemon juice
⅓ cup Amaretto
½ cup heavy cream
½ teaspoon salt (optional)
½ clove of garlic (optional)
Cooked and seasoned rice

SCALLOPS OREGANOTO

Melt butter in large skillet or sauté pan. Add scallops, pepper, garlic, parsley and oregano. Cook until scallops start to turn white. Add wine and lemon juice and simmer for 2 minutes. Add cubed tomatoes and mushrooms. Cook until thoroughly heated. Check seasoning and add salt, if desired. Serve with steaming rice or pasta. Garnish with sprigs of fresh oregano if available.

1 pound sea scallops
3 Tablespoons butter
½ teaspoon white pepper
1 teaspoon parsley, chopped
1 teaspoon oregano, chopped, ½ teaspoon if dried
Salt to taste
½ cup white wine
2 teaspoons lemon juice
2 tomatoes, cut in cubes
2 cups sliced mushrooms
Small clove of garlic (optional)
Fresh sprigs of oregano for garnish
Cooked pasta or rice

MARINATED SEAFOOD KABOBS

Beautiful on the grill as well as the broiler, they're excellent for entertaining because they can be made the day before.

Place seafood and vegetables on skewers, alternating meat and vegetables in any order you prefer. Mix all the marinade ingredients together until thoroughly blended. The bay leaves can be removed easily after standing 1 hour. Place kabobs in marinade for at least 15 minutes. Place kabobs on hot grill or broiler and cook for 10 to 15 minutes, or until seafood is white. Serve on a bed of seasoned rice or noodles.

Serves 6 to 8

MARINADE

1 cup vegetable oil
1 cup white wine
1 Tablespoon oregano
1 Tablespoon basil
1 Tablespoon thyme
3 bay leaves
½ teaspoon paprika
⅓ cup lemon juice

KABOBS

1 pound shrimp, peeled and deveined
1 pound scallops
1 pound lobster meat
2 onions, cut into 1" cubes
4 green or red peppers, cut into 1" cubes
1 pint cherry tomatoes
Prepared rice or noodles

5

POULTRY & STUFFINGS

POULTRY & STUFFINGS

A fancy dish called "wedding chicken" helped marry me to my career in the kitchen.

When my mother, aunt and I made it at home, we plucked the tender meat from plump roasting chickens, smothered it with a rich cream-flavored gravy and spooned it over flaky homemade patty shells.

Because it was special occasion fare, I wanted to use it on the first menu for Saturday night dinner guests who came to the farm in search of authentic Pennsylvania Dutch food. After all, anyone who took the time and trouble to find their way to Mount Joy deserved special treatment!

Before I could serve the dish, I knew I had to make a major modification. The patty shells had to go. Making those fragile morsels from scratch was such a labor-intensive task that just thinking about it tired me out.

To solve my problem, I took a hint from our practical Amish neighbors who routinely serve this chicken dish to 300 to 400 wedding guests at one seating. They make squares of biscuit dough to be placed under the chicken; I decided to serve mine with crisp but tender diamonds of buttery pastry.

When a writer asked me for a fancier name for the dish, I again thought of our Amish neighbors and gave it their name — Stoltzfus.

If ever there was a dish that turned to gold, this was it. And I attribute much of its success to saffron — the only extravagance you'll find in my recipes. The spice imparts a beautiful golden color to Chicken Stoltzfus. But more importantly, it imparts a flavor that's all its own. It's the kind of flavor that gives country cooking a name for itself.

Saffron, actually the red stamen from a special kind of purple crocus, has been called "the world's most expensive spice." We don't think of it that way because most of us grow our own. The bulbs are available from catalogs and some garden centers. They will multiply rapidly, provided no near-sighted gardener pulls them up (as mine does) and that no jealous rabbits divide them up for mid winter gourmet dinner.

We've developed many other good tasting poultry dishes for the Farm Restaurant and the Cameron Estate Inn, as you'll see in this chapter. In the years to come, we'll no doubt cook up many more, but they'll always be served in addition to Chicken Stoltzfus. I'm sure Chicken Stoltzfus will be served as long as there are Groffs in the kitchen.

CHICKEN STOLTZFUS AND PASTRY SQUARES

Named for our friends Elam and Hannah Stoltzfus, this has become one of the trademarks of Groff's Farm Restaurant. It is like the patty shells filled with chicken that were served to wedding guests at our family banquets, but are served like the Amish serve their "Wedding Chicken".

Put the chicken in a 6 quart kettle. Add the water, salt, pepper, and saffron and bring to a boil. Reduce the heat to medium and simmer, partially covered, for 1 hour. Remove the chicken and cool enough to debone. Strain the stock. Reduce the stock to 4 cups. Remove the skin and bones from the chicken and cut the meat into bite-sized pieces. Melt the butter in the pot in which the chicken was cooked and mix in the flour. Cook over medium-low heat until golden and bubbling. Add the 4 cups chicken stock and the cream, stirring constantly. Cook over medium-high heat until the sauce comes to a boil. Simmer until thickened and smooth. Reduce heat and add chicken pieces and chopped parsley. Serve hot over pastry squares.

1 (5 pound) roasting chicken, cleaned, giblets removed
1½ quarts water
2 teaspoons salt
⅓ teaspoon pepper
◆ Pinch of saffron
12 Tablespoons butter
12 Tablespoons flour
1 cup light cream or ½ cup each milk and evaporated milk
¼ cup finely chopped fresh or ⅛ cup dried parsley
Pastry Squares, see next page
Parsley for garnish

PASTRY SQUARES

These may be made beforehand. Store in an airtight container.

Cut the lard and butter into the flour and salt with a pastry blender, or mix by hand, until it forms crumbs. Sprinkle ice water over the crumbs with one hand, while tossing them lightly with the other hand. Use only enough water to hold the dough together. Press the dough into a ball and put on a lightly floured surface. Divide into 2 or 3 parts. Roll each part ⅛" thick to fit an ungreased cookie sheet. On the cookie sheets, cut the dough into 1" squares with a pastry wheel or sharp knife. Bake in a pre-heated 350° F. oven for 12 to 15 minutes until lightly browned. Arrange pastry squares on a heated platter. Spoon the chicken on top. Garnish with fresh parsley.

½ cup lard or vegetable shortening
½ cup butter
3 cups all-purpose flour
1 teaspoon salt
About ½ cup ice water

BRUNSWICK STEW

When doubled, this 'chicken stew' will feed a large family or a small crowd.

Melt the butter in a large kettle and lightly sauté the onions. Season the chicken pieces with salt and pepper and add to the pan along with the worcestershire, water, and tomatoes. Cover and cook for about 40 to 45 minutes until the meat is tender. Remove from the liquid and when cooled, debone, cutting the meat in bite size pieces. Add the potatoes to the broth and simmer for about 10 minutes before adding the limas, okra and corn. Cook an additional 10 to 15 minutes until the beans are tender. Add the crumbs, sugar and sherry and simmer for 10 more minutes. Check for seasoning and add additional if desired.

This also makes a delicious chicken pie if the broth is drained or reduced and the mixture is baked as a two crusted pie. Bake it in a preheated 375° F. oven for about 50 to 60 minutes until the top is golden brown. Be sure to make cuts in the top crust to allow the steam to escape.

Serves 8

6	pound chicken, cut up
1½	teaspoons salt
½	teaspoon pepper
2	Tablespoons butter
1	cup onion, chopped
1	Tablespoon worcestershire sauce
2½	cups water
16	ounces stewed tomatoes
4	potatoes, cut into 8 or 10 pieces each
2	cups lima beans, fresh or frozen
2	cups okra, fresh or frozen
2	cups corn, fresh or frozen
¾	cup fresh bread crumbs
1	Tablespoon sugar
½	cup sherry

MUMSIE'S CHICKEN CROQUETTES

These are especially good when topped with chicken gravy.

Melt the butter in a saucepan over low heat. Stir in the flour and gradually add the broth, stirring constantly. Add the salt, pepper and thyme and cook until the mixture is thick and creamy. Stir in the parsley and chicken and blend well. Remove from heat. Beat one of the eggs and add it to the chicken mixture. When blended in, return the pan to the heat again. Cook and stir for another minute or two. Remove from the heat and allow to cool until you can shape the mixture into croquettes. They can either be flat cakes, or pointed like a cone with a flat bottom. Beat the other egg with the milk and roll the shaped croquettes in the bread crumbs. Dip them in the egg mixture and roll in crumbs the second time. Allow them to stand in the refrigerator for about an hour before cooking. This will help them stay together. Heat corn oil in a deep skillet and fry, turning until light brown, deep fry for 3 minutes or bake in a preheated 375° F. oven for 25 to 30 minutes or until golden brown. If they've been fried, drain on paper toweling before serving.

3 Tablespoons butter or margarine
⅓ cup flour
1 cup chicken broth
1 teaspoon salt
1 teaspoon pepper
2 cups cooked chicken, finely diced
2 eggs
2 Tablespoons milk
1½ cups fine bread crumbs
½ teaspoon thyme (optional)
1 teaspoon chopped parsley (optional)

APPLE STUFFING

This stuffing is versatile! It goes equally well with poultry or fish, and is a delicious addition in stuffed pork chops.

Fry bacon and drain on paper towels. Break into bits. Sauté the celery, onion and parsley in the bacon fat for 10 minutes on low heat. Remove and place in a large mixing bowl. Add the sugar to the remaining fat in the pan. Add the apples and sauté, shaking the pan, until the apples are golden and almost soft. Put apples, bacon bits and cracker crumbs in the mixing bowl with the vegetables and toss together until well blended.

To stuff pork chops: Sauté them in butter until each side is golden brown, then fill with the apple stuffing. Place in a baking dish and bake in a preheated 350° F. oven for 45 minutes.

To stuff flounder fillets: Place apple stuffing in the middle of each fillet and overlap the ends. Turn them seam side down in the baking dish, pour 3 Tablespoons melted butter over the fish and bake in a preheated 350° F. oven for 30 minutes.

6 slices bacon
½ cup celery, chopped
¼ cup onion, chopped
¼ cup parsley, chopped
Freshly ground pepper
½ cup sugar
4 cups apples, peeled, cored and diced
1 cup cracker crumbs

WILD DUCK WITH CITRUS STUFFING AND GAME SAUCE

A domestic duck works just as well and is easier for most of us to get.

Rinse duck in cold water, pat dry, and sprinkle cavity with as much salt and pepper as desired. Cut the orange, apple, celery and onion and stuff the bird. If the duck is very lean, put the strips of salt pork or bacon over the breast while roasting. Place breast side up in a small roaster or baking dish and roast in a preheated 375° to 400° F. oven for about 1½ hours. Cover for the first half of the cooking time, then uncover and baste with the game sauce several times during the last 45 minutes.

1   duck, about 4 pounds
Salt and pepper to taste
1   orange, unpeeled and sliced
1   apple, unpeeled and sliced
1   cup celery, cut into 1"
      pieces
½   medium onion, sliced
4 to 6 strips of salt pork or bacon
      (optional)

Combine all of the above ingredients, beat, and allow to stand overnight in the refrigerator. Use ½ of the mixture for basting and serve the other half on the side, heated.

When using a wild duck, the stuffing is used to remove the wild game flavor. Some prefer to discard it or add it to the sauce.

Makes 1½ cups

GAME SAUCE

3   ounces frozen orange juice
      concentrate, undiluted
½   cup catsup
½   cup dry sherry
½   cup red currant jelly
◆ Dash of salt (optional)

CELERY STUFFING

Melt the butter in a skillet and lightly brown the onions. Add the celery and cook slightly, then stir in the lemon juice, parsley and saffron. Put the bread cubes in a bowl and toss lightly with the vegetable mixture, adding the broth last.

- 4 Tablespoons butter
- 1½ cups celery, chopped
- ¼ cup onion, chopped
- 1 Tablespoon lemon juice
- 1 Tablespoon parsley or chives
- ◆ Pinch of saffron
- 4 cups fresh bread cubes
- ½ cup broth, beef or chicken

CHESTNUT STUFFING

Chop the chestnuts — this can be done in a blender or food processor — and combine with the butter, cream, cracker crumbs, and salt and pepper to taste.

- 3 cups boiled or canned chestnuts, not water chestnuts
- ½ cup butter, melted
- ¼ cup light cream
- ½ cup saltine cracker crumbs
- Salt
- Freshly ground black pepper

ROAST CHICKEN WITH MOIST HERB STUFFING

Clean the chicken and rub the inside with salt. Stuff the chicken and close the opening with skewer and cord, truss, and rub the skin well with salt and pepper. Place in a roaster pan, cover, and cook in a preheated 375° F. oven for 3½ hours. Uncover for the last 15 minutes to brown the skin. Remove the chicken to a hot platter and keep warm.

Skim the fat from the pan juices, add 3 cups of water, and simmer to dissolve the browning. Thicken the gravy with cornstarch and water paste, and serve with the chicken and the stuffing.

6 pound roasting chicken
Salt and freshly ground pepper
Moist Herb Stuffing

MOIST HERB STUFFING

This is a good stuffing for those who are dieting or not using salt.

Put the bread cubes in a large bowl. Add the rest of the ingredients and toss lightly. Do not press the filling or it may become too heavy. Spoon into a generously buttered 2 quart baking dish and dot with butter. Bake in a preheated 350° F. oven for 30 to 40 minutes. When done, the tops of the cubes should be golden brown. Cover with foil to keep very hot until served. Use to stuff birds or pork chops or serve as an accompaniment to the main dish.

6 cups bread cubes
½ cup celery, chopped
1 teaspoon chervil, fresh or dried
1 teaspoon tarragon, fresh or dried
1 teaspoon parsley, fresh or dried
1 Tablespoon chives, fresh or dried
¼ cup onion
1 cup broth, chicken or beef
¼ teaspoon pepper
4 Tablespoons butter

EASY BROIL FRIED CHICKEN

Melt the butter in a broiler pan (remove the rack), so that you have a layer of butter about ¼" deep. Lay the chicken pieces in the butter, lightly salt and pepper them, with the bone side up. Broil until golden brown, turn, season the skin side, and broil until golden brown. Reduce oven heat to 350° F. and bake chicken for 15 minutes.

½ cup butter
3 frying chickens, cut in serving pieces
2 teaspoons salt
½ teaspoon freshly ground pepper

TURKEY TIMBALES

In a large mixing bowl, combine the turkey, celery, celery salt, lemon juice, parsley, white sauce, and salt. Form into cone-shaped croquettes. Roll in crumbs, then dip in beaten eggs and roll in crumbs again. Chill for at least 30 minutes until firm. Fry in preheated deep fat at 375° F. until golden brown. Keep warm in a preheated 300° F. oven until ready to serve. Serve very hot with turkey gravy. Garnish with fresh parsley.

Serves 4

1½ cups turkey, cooked and diced
¼ cup celery, finely chopped
¼ teaspoon celery salt
1 teaspoon lemon juice
1 teaspoon parsley, finely chopped
½ cup thick white sauce
½ teaspoon salt
2 cups crumbs, half bread and half saltine crackers
2 eggs, beaten
Fresh parsley for garnish

ROAST QUAIL IN CLAY

Our son John loved to hunt, and this was his favorite way to serve quail. His flair for the unusual presentation made this a show stopper. It is so much fun for the children, I recommend having them help to form their own clay birds, using the tip of the paring knife to scratch initials on the wings.

Carefully check home-hunted quail for shotgun pellets. Lightly pepper the quail or breasts. Take one breast at a time and press about ½ cup or more of the stuffing onto the bone side. Cover the stuffing with another breast, bone side in. Wrap a bacon strip tightly around the quail and secure the bacon by wrapping it in a lettuce leaf.

2 quail breasts or 1 whole quail per person
◆ **Dash of pepper for each**
Celery Stuffing, see Index
1 slice bacon for each quail
Lettuce leaves, patted dry for wrapping
Baking Clay (This is not edible.) See next page.

BAKING CLAY (This is NOT EDIBLE)

Mix the baking clay ingredients together and knead for about 5 minutes until very smooth. Roll out on a board, like pie pastry, and cut into 6 circles, 9″ in diameter, using a 9″ pie plate as a guide. Place the wrapped quail in the center of each circle of dough. Fold all the edges, using the ends to form the head and tail. A dab of water will help to make the clay more pliable. Water also seals the dough. Use whole cloves as the eyes, cut pieces of dough for wings. Brush off any excess flour and set, with sealed edges down, on a baking sheet or in a shallow baking pan. Bake in preheated 375° F. oven for 1¼ hours.

The clay becomes very hard, creating its own baking mold and retaining all the natural goodness inside. Have a large bowl or dish on the table for the broken clay. You may want to use wooden crab crackers to break open the clay. The clay may be rolled out and stored between waxed paper in the refrigerator if you want to have the clay prepared ahead of time.

4 cups flour
1 cup salt
1½ cups water

VARIATION

Cornish hen breasts may be substituted for quail.

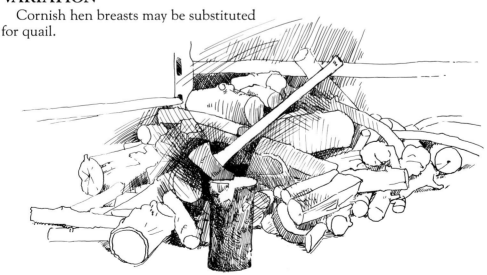

CHICKEN CAMERON

One of the Inn favorites, it is as beautiful to serve as it is easy to prepare.

Lay chicken breasts between waxed paper and pound thin. Mix bread crumbs and cheese together. Dip each piece of chicken in egg wash then in the crumb mixture. In large sauté pan or skillet, melt the butter and add the garlic. Place chicken in pan, season with salt and pepper. Brown on both sides, adding the almonds after turning (to prevent the almonds from burning). Remove the almonds when golden brown and set aside for serving. Add the lemon juice and wine and simmer for 5 minutes. Do not overcook! Place chicken on heated platter. Pour almonds and sauce over the chicken and garnish with lemon slices and capers.

4 chicken breasts, skinned and deboned
1½ cups bread crumbs
⅓ cup dried parmesan cheese
Egg wash (2 eggs, beaten lightly with ¼ cup milk)
4 Tablespoons butter
½ teaspoon coarsely ground pepper
Small clove of garlic, minced
1 cup sliced almonds
2 Tablespoons lemon juice
½ cup white wine
Lemon slices
Capers
½ teaspoon salt (optional)

VARIATION

Turkey breast may be substituted.

TARRAGON CHICKEN STRIPS

John's favorite recipe, he would make bucketsfull, eating as much as he possibly could, freezing the rest to reheat in the MICROWAVE.

Cut chicken into 1″ strips and roll in shortening, then in crushed corn flake crumbs. Place in a baking dish and sprinkle with pepper and tarragon. Bake in a pre-heated 350° F. oven for about 45 minutes until golden brown. Serve with your favorite dipping sauce.

2 chicken breasts, skin removed if desired
⅓ cup melted butter or corn oil
1 cup corn flakes, finely crushed
Freshly ground pepper
1 Tablespoon fresh tarragon, chopped or ½ Tablespoon dried

INDIVIDUAL CHICKEN LOAVES

For a different twist, try this recipe in individual baking cups or double it for a chicken loaf to slice.

Combine all of the above ingredients, the egg lightly beaten with the milk, the salt, pepper, worcestershire, rolled oats and celery with the diced chicken and mix thoroughly. Preheat the oven to 350° F. and pack the mixture into 6 greased custard cups. Place them in a pan and carefully fill with hot water no more than half way up the cup. Bake for 50 to 60 minutes or until nicely browned.

2 **cups chicken, cooked and diced**
1 **egg, beaten**
1 **cup milk**
1 **teaspoon salt**
½ **teaspoon pepper**
1 **Tablespoon worcestershire sauce**
1 **cup rolled oats, uncooked**
½ **cup celery, diced**

SMOKED TURKEY

One of my PM MAGAZINE shows used this recipe for an easy Memorial Day cookout. Try it with Apple Stuffing or one of your own favorites.

Remove giblets and use for stock. Rinse turkey in cold water and pepper inside and out, adding salt if desired. The herbs and pepper flavor the meat, making the salt unnecessary. When grill is hot, add wood chips or chunks which were soaked in water for 30 minutes. Put water pan in place and add 3 quarts of hot water, herbs and wine. Insert meat thermometer in center of thickest part of thigh with tip away from bone. Place turkey on grill and cover tightly with lid. Smoke-cook on medium heat for approximately 8 hours, checking the water pan from bottom of smoker every three hours. Add water when necessary, not filling the pan, but adding a cup of water at a time. You will want to use the juices in the pan for gravy or stock. EACH TIME YOU OPEN THE LID OF THE COOKER, YOU MUST ADD 20 MINUTES TO THE COOKING TIME. Remove and let cool a bit before serving if you want to serve it hot. This prevents the skin from breaking as you carve. If serving cold, cool for 1 hour before deboning, then refrigerate. Slice thin with very sharp knife or slicer, keeping all the little bits for turkey salad.

Use the directions from your grill or smoker-grill for exact timings.

1 (10 pound) turkey, fresh or thawed to room temperature
1 Tablespoon coarsely ground pepper
2 sprigs fresh rosemary or 1 teaspoon if dried
1 cup wine, apple juice or fruit juice of your choice
2 sprigs fresh tarragon or 1 teaspoon if dried
Salt (optional)

ROAST SQUAB OR CORNISH GAME HENS

Follow recipe and directions for seasoning and roasting in broaster bag, to keep the meat from drying out while baking, as given for Roast Pheasant. Baking time for squab should be 1 hour.

1 **bird per person**
Moist Bread Stuffing, see Index
Champagne Sauce, see Index

DUCK CHAMBORD

Roasting the ducks ahead of time is the secret of relaxed entertaining with this elegant recipe. For reheating, use the MICROWAVE since the duck is already browned. The sauce may be prepared ahead, too.

Place duck halves in shallow baking dish and season with salt and pepper. If you prefer a really crispy crust, score the skin at 1″ intervals. Bake in preheated 400° F. oven for 2 hours. Do not cover or baste. Remove from the oven and let cool enough to debone the breast. Debone, leaving the leg bones in place. Crush berries in food processor and pour into saucepan. Add liquor and bring to boil. Reheat duck in MICROWAVE for 10 minutes or place in heated oven for 20 minutes or until ready to serve. Pour some of the sauce over the duck and serve the rest on the side.

2 **ducks, 4 to 5 pounds each, split in half**
1 **teaspoon freshly ground pepper**
3 **cups black raspberries**
½ to 1 **cup raspberry liquor**
1 **teaspoon salt (optional)**

VARIATION

Use 2 Tablespoons honey, 1 Tablespoon mustard, ½ cup peach jam and ½ cup Peach Schnapps for sauce.

ROAST PHEASANT IN CHAMPAGNE SAUCE WITH CHESTNUT STUFFING

Fit for serving royalty, any hunter that passes up this recipe should think twice.

If using wild pheasant, remove any bullets that may have penetrated the meat. Some prefer to remove the skin, but it does make the meat drier. Place the stuffed pheasants in large, flour dusted broaster bag. Mix the salt, pepper, water, chervil and chives together and pour into bag. Seal and follow directions for baking. Place in baking pan and roast in 350° F. oven for 1½ hours. Drain the broth from bag and use for champagne sauce. Serve piping hot.

2   pheasants, fresh or frozen, approximately 1½ pounds each
Chestnut stuffing, see Index
Flour for dusting
1   teaspoon salt
½   teaspoon pepper
1½ cups water
1   teaspoon chervil, chopped
1   teaspoon chives, chopped
Champagne sauce

VARIATION

Roaster Chicken, Squab or Cornish Game Hens may be substituted. Stuff with your favorite stuffing and reduce the baking time to 1 hour for Squab or Cornish Game Hens.

CHAMPAGNE SAUCE (GRAVY)

This is a very versatile sauce. It is excellent with all poultry as well as fresh pork.

Melt butter in saucepan and stir in the flour. Simmer, stirring constantly, for a few minutes. Gradually add the broth and stir until smooth and thickened. Stir in the champagne and bring to a boil.

2   Tablespoons butter
4   Tablespoons flour
1½ cups chicken or beef broth, seasoned
1   cup champagne

6

MEATS

MEATS

I want to let you in on a little trade secret. If there's one thing that helps guarantee a cook's success in the kitchen, it is having a good relationship with the butcher.

You say no one has a relationship with a butcher in this day of supermarket display cases and impersonal service? That's simply not true. I have such a good relationship with one particular butcher that I kiss him every time I see him. Of course, that butcher happens to be my dad, and he has taught me much of what I know about quality meats and cooking them to bring out the best flavor.

Seriously, ring the bell or pick up the telephone at the supermarket meat counter. Someone cuts and packages those meats, you see, and he or she would probably love a little human contact.

My dad and my Uncle Emory were known for their country-cured smoked hams, dried beef, bacon and smoked sausage. Their smokehouse, scented with the aroma of burning hickory and apple chips and so thick with smoke that you couldn't see anything that was being smoked, can't be duplicated.

I love the memories and I like the idea of smoking meats to add extra flavor without adding extra calories, so I have been experimenting with a $60 backyard water smoker.

I wait until a weekend day when I'm not tired and assemble several different meats to be smoked at once. Sometimes, I'll do turkey and fish or beef and pork or whatever combination appeals to me at the time. Although the process requires some attention, the nuisance of smoking meats will be forgotten quickly when you taste the flavorful results and realize how much money you've saved by not having to pay the premium prices smoked meats command at the deli department of the grocery store.

Our family put everything to use, from pig's stomach (which was stuffed and baked) and sweetbreads to beef tongue and oxtails. Sausage, simply seasoned with ground pork and pepper, was cooked in apple cider to give it a tart flavor. Spareribs were barbecued long before they were trendy. I enjoyed almost everything except liver and even started liking it when I discovered how much better it tasted when it was still slightly pink. Stop short of overcooking it and you'll enjoy it more, too, whether it is simply pan fried or cooked with onions and wine glaze.

We also enjoyed the fancier cuts like the baked home cured hams, smothered pork chops, steaks, stuffed flank steaks and prime rib roasts. One of my favorites, particularly in spring, was stuffed pork chops. They're a delight when they're filled with

a savory bread stuffing. Apparently, however, they're a Pennsylvania specialty. When I tried to buy thick chops for stuffing in California, I got a very strange look from the local butcher who said he had heard of baking or grilling chops but never of stuffing them. Undaunted, I employed my be-nice-to-the-butcher strategy and he cut me all the thick chops I needed, complete with pockets.

FLANK STEAK WITH CELERY STUFFING

Stuff the flank steak with the stuffing and close the opening with skewers or sew with strong thread. Brown the meat in 3 Tablespoons cooking oil, then set on a rack 1″ high in a baking pan or dish. Add 2 cups water, cover with foil and bake in preheated 400° F. oven for ½ hour. Then, turn down to 350° F. and continue roasting for another hour and fifteen minutes. Allow the meat to cool for a few minutes, remove the skewers or thread, and slice on the diagonal. You may wish to double the stuffing recipe and bake one portion in a buttered casserole for the last hour or until the crumbs are golden brown on top.

1 **flank steak, approximately 1½ pounds**
2 **cups water**
Salt and pepper
Celery stuffing, see Index

BEEF STEAK WITH GREEN PEPPERCORNS

Charlie worked the grill at a steak house while he attended the Culinary Institute of America. He taught us a neat trick — you never pierce the meat, only touch it. The steak is like your thumb. Rare feels like the thickest part, medium is between the joints, and well-done is by the nail. It works every time no matter how thick the steak.

Blend butter and peppercorns in a mortar and pestle until smooth. Place the steaks on a hot grill or salted frying pan. Lightly salt the pan and heat till the salt dances. Add steaks at once, pressing the fat with a fork to melt it and brown the meat evenly. After turning the steaks, spread a dollop of the butter mixture on each steak and continue to cook to the degree of doneness you prefer.

4 **steaks, cut ½″ thick**
½ **cup butter**
1 **Tablespoon green peppercorns**

STANDING PRIME RIB ROAST

We always roast our standing prime rib in water. It keeps it moist and prevents shrinkage. Abe and Charlie have amazed even the best chefs with the consistency of the beef served at our restaurants.

Moisten the roast with water so the seasoning will stick. Sprinkle with the salt and pepper and place in a roasting pan. Add the water and tent loosely with foil. Bake in a preheated 275° F. oven for 4½ hours. To be sure the meat is cooked to your liking, use a meat thermometer. Remove the foil 35 minutes before serving to ensure even browning. When serving only the eye of the roast, save the rest for barbecued ribs, or to use for a rich stock. Trim the fat and cut away each rib separately for barbecued ribs. Use the sauce recipe for barbecued pork ribs (see Index), baking in a shallow pan at 425° F. until crispy.

MICROWAVE: Place standing rib roast fat side down on MICROWAVE rack in a 9″ x 13″ baking dish. Cover with paper towels and cook 5 minutes per pound for rare. After 25 minutes, remove from MICROWAVE and let stand for 5 minutes. Turn meat fat side up and cover again. Cook 15 minutes longer and remove from MICROWAVE. Cover with aluminum foil and let stand 25 minutes.

1 **6 pound prime or top choice standing rib roast**
2 **teaspoons salt, less if desired**
1 **teaspoon pepper**
1 **cup water**

VEGETABLE STUFFED FLANK STEAK

For a short cut, try this in your pressure cooker and cut the cooking time in half. Barb serves this by request of her daughters Lisa, Stephanie and Kristin.

Partially cook the bacon in a skillet or MICROWAVE for 4 to 5 minutes. Drain on paper towels and place in the pocket with the onions. Mix the carrots, turnips, and parsley with the salt and pepper and place on top of the bacon and onions. Close the pocket with two skewers or sew with heavy string and brown evenly on all sides in the oil. Put a rack in the bottom of a large saucepan and lay the meat on the rack. Add enough water to fill the pan to the bottom of the rack, but not cover the meat. Cover and simmer on top of the stove for 1½–2 hours or until meat is tender. The juices cooking out of the meat will flavor the water and they may be thickened for gravy. Taste for seasoning. If the broth is too weak, add a bouillon cube or two. You may wish to cook additional vegetables in the broth during the last half of the cooking time.

1 flank steak, about 1½ pounds, with a pocket
5 slices bacon
2 Tablespoons onion, chopped
½ cup carrots, grated
½ cup turnips, grated
3 Tablespoons fresh parsley, chopped
½ teaspoon salt
½ teaspoon freshly ground pepper
1 Tablespoon cooking oil

PEPPER STEAK

"Mike" Capatch, one of my cooking school students, shared this favorite with our class. I like it as much as the red Corvette I purchased from her husband.

Sprinkle meat with paprika and allow to stand while preparing other ingredients. Using a large skillet, brown meat in butter. Add garlic and broth. Cover and simmer for 30 minutes, then stir in onions and green peppers. Cover and cook for 5 more minutes. Blend the cornstarch, water and soy sauce together and stir into the meat mixture. Cook, stirring until clear and thickened, about 2 minutes. Add tomatoes, including juice, and stir gently. Serve over rice.

1	pound lean beef round steak, cut into ½" x 2" pieces
1	Tablespoon paprika
2	Tablespoons butter
2	cloves garlic, crushed
1½	cups beef broth
1	cup green onions, sliced
2	green peppers, cut in strips
2	Tablespoons cornstarch
¼	cup soy sauce
¼	cup water
2	large fresh tomatoes or 16 ounces, canned
3	cups hot, cooked rice

MEAT LOAF

This has to be one of America's all time favorite foods. Who doesn't remember their Mother's meat loaf?

Mix the ground chuck and veal together, then add the eggs, salt, pepper, 1 cup of crumbs, juice, worcestershire sauce, onion and celery and mix thoroughly. Form into a loaf and place in a baking dish. Bake in a preheated 350° F. oven for an hour and 15 minutes, then sprinkle the remaining ¼ cup of crumbs mixed with butter on top and return to the oven for another 15 minutes until the crumbs are slightly browned. Allow the meat loaf to rest about 15 minutes before slicing.

1½	pounds ground chuck
1	pound ground veal
2	eggs, lightly beaten
1	teaspoon salt
¾	teaspoon freshly ground pepper
1¼	cups fresh bread crumbs
¾	cup vegetable juice
1	Tablespoon worcestershire sauce
¼	cup onion, chopped
½	cup celery, chopped
2	Tablespoons butter

MEATBALLS IN SOUR CREAM GRAVY

Barb's grandmother, Mumsie, was known as an excellent cook in her home counties of Somerset and Huntingdon, Pennsylvania. This was one of her favorite ways to turn ground chuck into a "company" dinner.

If using corn flakes, crush into fine crumbs and combine with the meat, milk, salt, pepper, and onions and mix thoroughly. Shape into 2″ balls around an olive. Melt the shortening in a skillet and put the meatballs in it, turning them to brown evenly. Remove to a platter and pour off all but 3 Tablespoons of the brownings. Blend in the flour, then the water and stir constantly until smooth and thickened. Stir in the sour cream, dill and ¼ teaspoon salt and add the browned meatballs. Cover and cook slowly on low heat for 20 to 25 minutes. Serve over hot, buttered noodles. More salt may be desired by some cooks, but the addition of green olives makes it unnecessary.

Makes 20 to 22, 2″ meatballs

2 pounds ground chuck
4 cups corn flakes, crushed or 1 cup packaged corn flake crumbs
1 cup milk
1 teaspoon salt
½ teaspoon pepper
½ cup onions, chopped
20 large green or ripe pitted olives
3 Tablespoons shortening
3 Tablespoons flour
½ cup water
2 cups sour cream
1 teaspoon dill seed
¼ teaspoon salt

REUBEN CROQUETTES

By making these smaller, they serve as a hearty appetizer.

Drain the sauerkraut and press out as much juice as possible. Chop the sauerkraut, onions and corned beef very fine. This can be done in a blender or food processor. Add two eggs, rice, cheese, salt and pepper. Mix and shape into approximately 25 croquettes, ¼ cup each, or 18 larger ones. Combine the other 2 eggs with the water and beat with a fork. Roll each shaped croquette into the crumbs, then the egg, and then the crumbs again. Let them stand for a half hour in the refrigerator so they stick together better. Fry in shallow oil in a skillet for 5 to 7 minutes, turning to brown, or bake on a greased cookie sheet in a preheated 425° F. oven for 20 to 30 minutes, depending on the size of the croquette. Heat mustard sauce slowly. Serve over the croquettes.

1 pound sauerkraut
1 small onion
12 ounce can of corned beef
4 eggs
2 cups cooked rice
1 cup Swiss cheese
1 teaspoon salt
¼ teaspoon pepper
3 Tablespoons water
2 cups fine, dry bread crumbs
   or corn flake crumbs
Mustard Sauce, see below

MUSTARD SAUCE

Combine all ingredients and heat slowly. Serve over Reuben Croquettes or with ham.

¾ cup mayonnaise
¼ cup milk
1 Tablespoon lemon juice
3 Tablespoons prepared
   mustard

SHEPHERD'S PIE

A new version of an old recipe, this is a good way to use leftover roasts.

Make mashed potatoes and set aside. In a saucepan sauté the meats in butter, then remove from pan. Lightly brown the onions in the drippings, add the broth and flour and stir until smooth and thickened. Add the worcestershire, thyme, marjoram, peas and pimento and simmer for 10 minutes. Grease a 2 quart casserole and add the meat mixture. Put the potatoes in a pastry bag with a large star tip and pipe them around the edge of the dish. Sprinkle with paprika and bake in a preheated 400° F. oven for 30 minutes or until lightly browned.

Mashed Potato recipe, see Index
2 **Tablespoons butter or vegetable oil**
Medium onion, chopped
1½ **cups lean pork, cooked and cut in 1" cubes**
1½ **cups lean beef, cooked and cut in 1" cubes**
2 **cups pork or beef broth or leftover gravy**
4 **Tablespoons flour**
1 **Tablespoon worcestershire sauce**
1 **teaspoon thyme**
1 **teaspoon marjoram**
2 **cups frozen peas**
¼ **cup pimento, sliced**
Paprika and fresh parsley to garnish

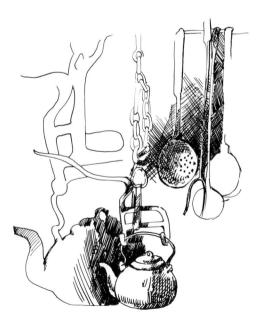

CHEESE STEAKS WITH SAUCE

For ease in slicing, place the steak in the freezer until almost firm.

In a skillet, melt the butter and sauté the onions until lightly browned. Remove them from the pan and add the beef, sliced very thin. Cook until the red disappears, stirring often. Turn off the heat, cover, and let stand until the sauce is ready. In a saucepan, combine the catsup, honey, mustard, vinegar, tabasco, cinnamon, nutmeg, and pepper and simmer for 5 to 10 minutes. Lightly toast the split rolls if desired. Sprinkle some cheese on the roll, top with meat, then more cheese. Serve the sauce on the side or on top of the meat before the cheese topping.

2 Tablespoons butter or vegetable oil

Medium onion, chopped

1½ pounds beef steak or ground chuck

Salt and pepper to taste

½ cup catsup

1 Tablespoon honey

1 Tablespoon mustard

1 Tablespoon tarragon vinegar

◆ Dash of tabasco

◆ Dash of cinnamon

◆ Dash of nutmeg

◆ Dash of coarsely ground pepper

6 steak rolls

1½ cups cheddar or longhorn cheese, shredded

BEEF TIPS WITH NOODLES

Melt the butter in a skillet and sauté the beef cubes until lightly browned. Season with salt and pepper. Remove the meat and add the onions, chives and mushrooms and cook for 5 minutes. Add ½ cup wine or water to deglaze the pan. When heated, stir in the sour cream and add the beef cubes, sitrring until smooth and heated thoroughly. Serve over noodles.

2 **Tablespoons butter or vegetable oil**
2 **pounds boneless cubed beef, rump or loin**
1 **teaspoon salt**
¼ **teaspoon pepper**
¼ **cup onion, chopped**
¼ **cup fresh chives, chopped**
½ **cup red wine**
1½ **cups sour cream**
1 **cup sliced mushrooms (optional)**

VEAL STEAKS IN CREAM

Arrange slices of bacon in skillet to cover bottom. Top with onion rings and herbs and sauté until limp. Add veal steaks and simmer on medium heat until veal and bacon are golden brown. Remove the veal and bacon to heated platter. Skim the fat and discard the herbs. Add flour, vinegar, salt and pepper to brownings and stir until blended. Gradually add milk and sour cream and heat until thickened into a brown sauce. Pour over the veal and serve with rice.

1½ pounds veal cutlets or steaks, cut ½" thick
6 slices bacon
Medium onion, sliced in rings
Herb bouquet: 1 sprig each — rosemary, thyme and parsley
2 Tablespoons flour
1 teaspoon tarragon vinegar
½ teaspoon salt
1 teaspoon freshly ground pepper
½ cup milk
½ cup sour cream

LAMB CHOPS WITH TARRAGON

In a large skillet, melt the butter and brown the chops on each side until golden brown. Remove the chops to a heated platter. Sprinkle salt, pepper, flour and tarragon over the brownings. Slowly add the wine, stirring until smooth. Add the milk and stir until thickened. Add chops to sauce and simmer for several minutes. Serve extra sauce in a gravy boat. Garnish chops with fresh tarragon.

3 Tablespoons butter or oil
2 chops per person
◆ Dash of salt
◆ Dash of pepper
1 Tablespoon flour
1 Tablespoon fresh tarragon, chopped
⅓ cup white wine
½ cup half-and-half or 2% milk for fewer calories
Fresh tarragon for garnish

GRILLED HAM STEAK

Cut slashes every 2″ around the outer edge of the ham slice so that it will lay flat. Place on a hot grill and cook for 10 to 12 minutes or until nicely browned. Turn over and spread the top of the slice with the Honey-Mustard Sauce. Grill for another 10 to 12 minutes. Serve with extra sauce.

Smoked ham slice, 1″ thick
Honey-Mustard Sauce

HONEY-MUSTARD SAUCE

Mix the two mustards together making sure there are no lumps, then add the mayonnaise, sour cream and the honey.

¼ cup dijon mustard
1 teaspoon dry mustard
¼ cup mayonnaise
2 Tablespoons sour cream
2 Tablespoons honey

PORK POT PIE

Brown all sides of the pork roast in a dutch oven or large stockpot. Cover with 7 cups of water. Boil meat until tender, approximately 2 hours. Remove and debone. Skim fat from the broth. If you do not have 6 cups of broth add water or chicken broth. Add vegetables. Bring the broth and vegetables to a boil over high heat. Drop the pot pie squares into the broth in layers, being careful not to put in a second layer until the boiling broth has covered the first one. As the pot gets full, take a fork and push the squares down. Cook until the squares are tender, about 10 to 12 minutes; then add the pieces of pork, cover and simmer for 5 minutes, until heated through. Serve the pot pie, meat and broth in bowls.

VARIATION

Chicken Pot Pie is my favorite. Substitute roaster chicken for pork.

3 pounds fresh pork roast with bone

1 teaspoon salt, more or less if desired

6 cups pork broth, chicken broth may be added to make 6 cups

1 cup celery with leaves, corsely chopped

1 cup peeled potatoes, sliced thin or cubed

½ cup onion, coarsely chopped

1 Tablespoon parsley, chopped

1 teaspoon coarsely ground pepper

½ teaspoon thyme

½ teaspoon marjoram

Pot Pie Dough, see Index

POT PIE DOUGH

Pot Pie is equally good with ham, beef or chicken.

Mound the flour on a pastry board or marble slab and make a well in the center. Break the eggs into the well and add the water, butter and salt. Gradually mix the flour into the other ingredients until well blended. Gather into a ball and knead the dough until it is very tender, smooth and elastic. Generously flour the board and roll out the dough very thin, no more than $\frac{1}{8}''$ thick; the thinner you roll it, the more delicate it will be. Cut in 2″ squares and boil in broth until done.

2½ cups flour
2 eggs
⅓ cup water
1 Tablespoon butter
½ teaspoon salt

HAM-STUFFED CABBAGE ROLLS

Rinse cabbage. Cut out the core and remove the outer two or three leaves from the head. Save them and any other leaves that are torn or too small and cover the bottom of a large saucepan or Dutch oven. This will help prevent the cabbage rolls from sticking while cooking. Place the cabbage in a casserole dish and MICROWAVE on high for 8 minutes in ½" of water, covered with wax paper. Drain. When cool enough, remove the outer 12 to 16 leaves and cut off the thick rib at the back of each leaf. Combine the meat, rice, crumbs, eggs, onions, pineapple, salt and pepper and mix well with your hands. Divide into 12 to 16 equal balls and flatten them slightly in the center of each leaf. Fold the sides in and overlap the top and bottom securely, then place seam side down in the saucepan. Top with Orange-Pineapple Sauce and simmer, covered, for an hour or longer. Serve with additional rice on the side if desired.

Serves 6 to 8

2½ pound head of cabbage
2 pounds smoked ham, ground
1 cup cooked rice
1 cup dried bread crumbs
2 eggs, lightly beaten
½ cup onion, I prefer 6 or 7 green (Spring) onions
½ cup crushed pineapple
Salt and pepper to taste
Orange-Pineapple Sauce, see below

ORANGE-PINEAPPLE SAUCE

Mix sugar and cornstarch together and stir into the juices. Heat, stirring constantly until clear and thickened, then add coloring, if desired, and fruit. Add more of either juice if extra liquid is needed.

4 Tablespoons sugar
2 Tablespoons cornstarch
1½ cups orange juice
1½ cups pineapple juice
1 cup pineapple tidbits
◆ Few drops red food coloring (optional)

BAKED HOME-CURED HAM

Remove the rind from the cured ham and place, bone side down, in a roaster pan. Add water, tent with foil, and bake in a preheated 300° F. oven for 2½ hours. Remove and debone. If the broth seems salty, pour off and add 2 cups fresh water. Put the deboned ham in the water and continue to bake at 300° F. for another hour. Baking the ham in water keeps it moist and tender. Changing the water is necessary only if the ham is very salty. It will still retain the smoky flavor.

12 to 14 pound whole smoked, cured ham
2 cups water

VARIATION

Glaze the ham while baking with grape, cherry or plum jelly.

HAM, GREEN BEANS AND NEW POTATOES

Place the ham hock and water in a 4 quart Dutch oven or large saucepan with a lid. Bring to a boil and cook until meat falls from the bones. Remove meat, trim fat and cut into bite size pieces. Add scrubbed, unpeeled potatoes to broth and cook until tender, approximately 20 minutes. Add beans and simmer for 15 minuts or longer. Return meat to the pan and serve when heated thoroughly.

1 ham hock
4 cups green beans, whole or cut
6 cups water
12 new potatoes, medium size
Salt and pepper to taste

SCRAPPLE

Once a winter favorite, but now a favorite all year round, this was always made with all the bone cuts after the loins, steaks, roasts and hams were finished. Butchering the hogs for the season was a big family project. Nothing was wasted and each family member had their own jobs and specialties. As a child, I deboned the cooked meat and removed the gristle for the scrapple. Now we have pork available all the time, so you can make it often. It is usually considered a breakfast food, but I prefer it as a lunch or supper dish. It must be sliced thin and fried crisp. We always used golden table molasses on top but most folks like it with syrup or better yet, real maple syrup.

In large stockpot, add water, pork bone pieces, salt, pepper and herbs. Bring to a boil and simmer for 3 hours or until the meat falls away from the bone. Remove the bones and meat and strain the broth. Debone and remove the fat and gristle. Chop the meat in a food processor or grinder, making sure you have at least 2½ cups chopped meat. Skim most of the fat from the broth, making sure you have at least 3 quarts of broth. If not, add water to make 3 quarts. Place broth and meat in heavy pot and bring to a boil. Slowly add the corn meal, stirring constantly with whisk to prevent lumping of corn meal. Simmer on low heat for 1 hour, stirring occasionally. It should be thick like mush. Pour into loaf pans and cool. Refrigerate (it does freeze well) until ready to serve. Slice ⅓ inch thick and fry until golden and crisp on each side. Some prefer to dredge each slice in flour, then fry in greased pan.

Serve with syrup or molasses.

4 **quarts water**
Pork rib rack
Pork heart and pig's feet (optional); sausage meat may be substituted
2 **teaspoons salt**
2 **teaspoons coarsely ground pepper**
½ **teaspoon basil**
◆ **Pinch of rosemary**
◆ **Pinch of thyme**
3½ **cups corn meal**

BARBECUED SPARERIBS

Some people bake their ribs but I prefer boiling mine. It gets rid of excess fat, and makes them even more tender.

Sprinkle the ribs with salt and pepper and place in a large shallow saucepan. Add water to the top of the ribs, but not covering the meat, and boil until all of the water dries up, approximately 45 minutes. In another pan, heat the bacon drippings and stir in the onion and garlic. Cook over medium heat for two minutes, stirring constantly. Mix in the finely ground beef and cook, stirring until the meat begins to brown. Combine the catsup, vinegar, remaining salt, paprika, mustard, worcestershire, chili powder, tabasco and sugar in a small bowl and add to the meat mixture. Stir constantly over low heat until the mixture thickens. Pour over the ribs, cover with foil and bake in a preheated 325° F. oven for an hour.

3 pounds spareribs
1 teaspoon salt
¼ teaspoon pepper
3 Tablespoons bacon drippings
¼ cup onion, finely chopped
1 clove garlic, mashed
1 pound lean ground chuck, finely ground
1 cup catsup
3 Tablespoons cider vinegar
½ teaspoon salt
2 teaspoons paprika
1 Tablespoon prepared mustard
¼ cup worcestershire sauce
1 teaspoon chili powder
1 teaspoon tabasco sauce
⅔ cup brown sugar

SMOTHERED PORK CHOPS

Another favorite from Alice Brennan.

Wipe the chops and sprinkle with salt and pepper. Coat with pancake mix. Heat oil in a large skillet and brown chops well on both sides. Remove from skillet to a shallow roasting pan. Sauté onions with the remaining salt, pepper and sugar in the same skillet until lightly browned. Stir in flour and cook until well blended. Gradually add boiling water. Cook over medium heat stirring constantly until the sauce boils and thickens. Pour over the chops. Cover pan tightly with foil and bake in a preheated 350° F. oven for one hour and 20 minutes. Remove chops to serving platter; keep warm. Strain gravy through a sieve if desired, pressing onions through with a wooden spoon. Skim fat from surface of gravy, if necessary. Serve each chop with a generous portion of the gravy.

6 center-cut pork chops, 1" thick
1 teaspoon salt
¼ teaspoon coarse pepper
¼ cup pancake mix
3 Tablespoons vegetable oil
2 medium onions, sliced (can use less if preferred)
1 teaspoon salt
¼ teaspoon white pepper
1 Tablespoon sugar
¼ cup all-purpose flour
2 cups boiling water

SAUSAGE AND CHEESE TARTS

A perfect brunch or light supper entrée. These tarts are quick to make and the flavor is easily changed by using different kinds of cheese.

Brown the loose sausage in a skillet and drain off the excess fat. Combine the biscuit mix, butter and boiling water and mix into a soft dough. Divide the dough into 12 small balls and press into the bottom of greased muffin cups. Divide sausage evenly on top of each cup. Lightly beat the egg with the milk and add the onion. Pour this over the meat and top with equal portions of the cheese. Bake in a preheated 350° F. oven for 25 to 30 minutes, until golden brown.

Makes 12 tarts

½ pound pork sausage
1½ cups packaged biscuit mix
¼ cup butter or margarine, softened
3 Tablespoons boiling water
1 egg, slightly beaten
½ cup light cream or milk
3 Tablespoons green onion, thinly sliced
1½ cups shredded cheese — (Jarlsberg, cheddar or swiss)

SAUSAGE IN CIDER

Tom and Betty Hooker shared this, their most favorite recipe. You can't believe how good it is until you try it, too. Thanks, friends!

Put the sausage in a skillet, prick each link several times with a fork, and cover them with water. Cook for 10 minutes, then uncover and let the liquid cook off until the meat is browned all around. Place in a warm oven. Add the butter to the same skillet and lightly brown the onions and celery. Add the parsley, chives, and flour. Mix well to blend and add the cider. Stir constantly until the mixture comes to a boil and is smooth and thickened. Add the chopped apple last and simmer for 4 minutes; put the sausage back in the pan. Serve while the apples are still semi-soft, not mushy.

- 1 **pound fresh sausage links**
- ¼ **cup water**
- 3 **Tablespoons butter**
- 2 **Tablespoons onion, chopped**
- 1 **teaspoon parsley, chopped**
- ⅓ **cup celery, chopped**
- 1 **teaspoon chives**
- 1 **Tablespoon flour**
- 1 **cup cider**
- 1 **apple, chopped (a sweet Red or Yellow Delicious)**

GRANDMA'S GLAZED HAM BALLS

They don't come much easier than this recipe! You don't even brown the meat, the oven does the work for you.

Mix the ham and pork together, then add the eggs, crumbs and milk. Form into 18, 2″ balls. They can be smaller for appetizers. Place the ham balls in a shallow baking dish. Mix the brown sugar, mustard, vinegar, water and food coloring together and pour over the meat. Bake in a preheated 325° F. oven for an hour or longer, basting every 15 minutes.

- 1 **pound ham, finely ground**
- 1½ **pounds pork, finely ground**
- 2 **eggs, well beaten**
- 2 **cups fresh bread crumbs**
- 1 **cup milk**

GLAZE
- 1 **cup brown sugar**
- 1 **teaspoon dry mustard**
- ½ **cup vinegar**
- ½ **cup water**
- **Few drops red food coloring**

GLAZED HAM LOAF WITH HORSERADISH SAUCE

Mix the meats together in a bowl then add the crumbs, eggs, milk, water, pepper, mustard and worcestershire and mold into a loaf when thoroughly blended. Bake in a preheated 350° F. oven for an hour and a half. Make a sauce of the vinegar, sugar, syrup and juice, and baste frequently while the ham loaf is baking. About 15 minutes before the meat is done, garnish the top of the loaf with as many orange sections as desired and glaze again. The meat should rest for 15 minutes before being sliced. Mix the whipped cream, horseradish and mayonnaise together and serve on the side.

1 pound ham, ground
½ pound pork, ground
½ pound ground chuck
1 cup fresh bread crumbs
2 eggs
½ cup evaporated milk
½ cup water
Coarsely ground pepper to taste
1 teaspoon prepared mustard
1 teaspoon worcestershire sauce

GLAZE

2 Tablespoons vinegar
¼ cup brown sugar
2 Tablespoons maple syrup
¾ cup Mandarin orange juice
Mandarin orange sections to garnish

SAUCE

⅓ cup cream, whipped
1 Tablespoon horseradish
1 Tablespoon mayonnaise

STUFFED PORK CHOPS

Definitely a Pennsylvania Dutch specialty worth trying.

Simmer the apricots, celery, half of the butter and water in a covered saucepan about 5 minutes or until the celery is tender. Toss together with the bread cubes and divide the mixture, stuffing the chops. Use a skewer or toothpicks to keep them closed and season with salt and pepper. Melt 2 Tablespoons of butter in an oven-proof skillet and brown the chops on both sides. Spoon the applesauce over the chops and sprinkle with the raisins. Cover and bake in a preheated 350° F. oven for 30 minutes. Uncover and continue cooking for another 15 minutes.

6 center loin pork chops, cut 1½" thick with a pocket
½ cup dried apricots, cut in thin strips
½ cup celery, finely chopped
4 Tablespoons butter
⅓ cup water
2 cups soft bread cubes
Salt and pepper to taste
1½ cups applesauce
½ cup raisins

PORK CHOPS AND ORANGE RICE

Brown both sides of the chops in butter and remove to a platter. In the same skillet, lightly brown the celery, mushrooms and onions and remove them. Cook rice according to the instructions, substituting orange juice for ½ cup water. Butter and salt may be omitted. Add one beef bouillon cube and one chicken if desired for stronger flavor. As the rice cooks, more orange juice and more water may be added to get it to the desired consistency. Mix the cooked vegetables, chervil and pepper into the rice and place in a long baking dish that has been sprayed with cooking oil. Place the chops on top of the rice, cover with foil and bake in a preheated 350° F. oven for 45 minutes. Uncover, and continue baking for another 15 minutes.

6 ½" thick loin pork chops
2 Tablespoons butter
1 cup celery, sliced
1 cup mushrooms, sliced (6 or 7 large)
½ cup onion, chopped
2 cups instant rice
1½ cups water
½ cup orange juice concentrate
1 beef bouillon cube
1 chicken bouillon cube (optional)
1 teaspoon chervil
Coarsely ground pepper

ROAST PORK LOIN WITH BRANDIED FRUIT SAUCE

This makes an ordinary roast a treat for the eye as well as the palate.

Season the pork with salt and pepper and place in small roasting pan. Add water and tent with foil. Bake in preheated 375° F. oven for 2 hours. Remove from oven and add juice from the brandied fruit sauce, baking an additional 15 minutes uncovered. Place fruit on roast and bake until fruit is thoroughly heated. Serve with remainder of the sauce on the side.

MICROWAVE: Bake in glass baking dish for approximately 36 minutes, covered with waxed paper. Let stand in oven for approximately 15 minutes before adding glaze. If your microwave does not brown, place under regular broiler until golden brown.

3 pound pork loin or roast
½ teaspoon salt
½ teaspoon coarsely ground pepper
½ cup water
Foil for tent cover
Brandied Fruit Sauce, see below

BRANDIED FRUIT SAUCE

This may be used for any roast such as chicken, ham or whole fish.

Remove pits from prunes. Place dried fruits and water or juice in large saucepan. Bring to a boil and simmer for 15 minutes, pressing the apple slices down into the broth, stirring occasionally. Add brandy and nutmeg and bring to a boil.

2½ cups or 11 ounces mixed dried fruits
2½ cups water or fruit juice
⅓ cup brandy or peach schnapps
½ teaspoon nutmeg

CURRANT-GLAZED LEG OF LAMB

Sprinkle the lamb with salt and pepper. Place on a rack in a roasting pan. Roast in a preheated 325° F. oven for 20 to 25 minutes per pound, or until a meat thermometer registers 145° F. for medium-rare doneness. Meanwhile, combine the sherry, jelly, catsup, and marjoram in a small saucepan and stir over low heat until the jelly melts. Brush the lamb frequently with the sauce during the last 1½ hours of roasting time. Heat the remaining sauce and serve with the lamb. Garnish with parsley and lemon wedges.

1 leg of lamb, 6–9 pounds
Salt and pepper
½ cup dry sherry
½ cup red currant jelly
½ cup catsup
½ teaspoon dried marjoram
Parsley
Lemon wedges

LAMB CHOPS WITH MUSHROOM SAUCE

Dave, our chef at the Farm, developed this for his first contribution. We all love it.

Remove the skin and trim the extra fat from the chops, slashing at 1″ intervals around the curved part of the chop so the meat won't curl. Combine the salt, pepper, thyme, oregano, basil and rosemary and sprinkle the meat. Melt the butter and brown the chops quickly on both sides in a very hot skillet. Remove to a platter. Add the onions and mushrooms to the drippings and cook for a few minutes. Remove them and deglaze the pan with ¼ cup red wine. Add the roux and gradually stir in the beef broth and browning sauce until thickened. Season with salt and pepper to taste. Finish cooking the chops in the broiler, 3 to 4 minutes for rare, 6 minutes for medium, and 7 to 8 minutes for well-done. Top with the sauce and garnish. Serve with Baked Apple-Mint Slices (see Index).

8 6-ounce lamb chops, 1″ thick
2 Tablespoons butter
1 teaspoon salt
½ teaspoon pepper
½ teaspoon thyme
½ teaspoon oregano
½ teaspoon basil
◆ Pinch rosemary
⅓ cup onions, finely chopped
1 heaping cup mushrooms
¼ cup red wine
2 Tablespoons roux (½ butter, ½ flour)
1 teaspoon browning sauce such as Kitchen Bouquet
2 cups beef broth
Salt and white pepper to taste
Garnish with a sprig of mint, fresh parsley or fresh rosemary

BEEF TONGUE

You've heard the old saying, "My wife serves me cold tongue"? Well, here goes — — enjoy!

Place the tongue in a stockpot, cover with water, and add the pepper, celery, parsley, thyme, salt and pepper and bring to a boil. Reduce heat to medium and cover partially with a lid. Simmer until tender, approximately 3 hours. Let cool in broth, peel and chill. Serve sliced thin with Horseradish Sauce, see below.

If smoking, place on rack over wet wood chips, keeping the heat very low. To prevent drying out, place a pan of water over the wood chips. For cooking time, see the instructions with your smoker grill.

1 beef tongue
1 green pepper
4 ribs celery
1 Tablespoon parsley
½ teaspoon thyme
2 teaspoons salt
1 teaspoon coarsely ground pepper

HORSERADISH SAUCE

Fold the horseradish and mayonnaise into the whipped cream. This is especially good with Ham Loaf.

⅓ cup heavy cream, whipped
1 Tablespoon horseradish
1 Tablespoon mayonnaise

BRAISED OXTAIL

I always looked forward to our weekly supper of oxtail. It was considered ordinary and never served to guests. What a surprise when the Culinary Team from Denmark served Braised Oxtail as one of their entrées at the Culinary Olympics in Frankfurt, Germany. It is great to see our regional foods elevated to such heights by those studying food around the world.

Have the butcher cut the tails at each joint, cutting half way through. Place in a stockpot and cover with water, about 2½ quarts. Add the rest of the ingredients — celery, salt, chives, pepper and vinegar — cover with a lid, and bring to a boil. Cook on medium heat for three hours. Let cool in broth. Remove fat from the meat. Place under broiler until heated and edges are crisp. Serve with winter root vegetables such as turnips, parsnips, salsify, sweet potatoes, etc.

2 oxtails
½ cup onion, chopped
3 ribs celery
3 teaspoons salt
1 teaspoon chopped chives
1 teaspoon peppercorns, crushed
1 teaspoon wine vinegar

LIVER, ONIONS AND BACON WITH WINE GLAZE

Fry the bacon in a skillet, or cook in a MICROWAVE until golden brown, and drain on paper towels. Brown the onions in the bacon drippings until they're soft and golden. Remove them with a slotted spoon and reserve with the bacon. Add the 2 Tablespoons of butter to the drippings to make 4 Tablespoons of oil. Dredge the liver in the flour and sauté over moderate heat until it's browned on both sides. It should be slightly pink in the center. Don't overcook. Remove the liver and pour the wine into the skillet, simmer for about 5 minutes to reduce the liquid. Return the liver and onions to the skillet and simmer for another minute or two. Serve each portion of liver topped with a little sauce and some crumbled bacon.

1 pound liver, sliced
6 slices bacon
1 medium onion, sliced
½ cup flour
2 Tablespoons butter
1 cup white wine
Salt and pepper to taste

SAUTÉED SWEETBREADS ELEGANTE

Veal sweetbreads are more tender, delicate and expensive than beef sweetbreads, but both are wonderful.

Precook sweetbreads in large saucepan in 1 quart of water, 1 teaspoon salt and 1 Tablespoon lemon juice or vinegar. The acid keeps the sweetbreads white and firm. Simmer for 20 minutes. Remove and rinse under cold water, slipping off the membranes with fingers. Cut out any dark veins and connective tissue. Cut meat into bite sized chunks and dredge in flour. Melt butter in large sauté pan, adding salt, pepper, mustard and floured sweetbreads. Sauté until golden brown on one side and add almonds, onions and mushrooms. When golden brown on both sides, add white wine. Stir in the heavy cream and check for seasonings. Add more pepper and salt if desired and simmer for a few minutes until thickened. Serve on toast tips and parsley.

Serves 4

1 pound veal or beef sweetbreads, precooked in salt and lemon juice or vinegar

Flour for dredging

4 Tablespoons butter

½ teaspoon salt

½ teaspoon white pepper

½ teaspoon dry mustard

⅓ cup almonds, slivered

½ cup onion, chopped

1 cup mushrooms, sliced

⅓ cup white wine

¾ cup heavy cream or half-and-half

Toast tips

Parsley

VEAL SIMON CAMERON

Place veal cutlets between waxed paper and pound thin. Mix bread crumbs and cheese together. Dip each piece of veal in egg wash, then the crumb mixture. In large sauté pan or skillet, melt the butter and add the garlic. Place the veal in pan and season with salt, pepper, basil and chervil. Brown on both sides but do not overcook. Add the lemon juice and wine and simmer for 5 minutes. Place veal on heated platter and top with the wine sauce. Garnish with lemon slices and capers.

VARIATION

Chicken or turkey may be substituted.

1 pound veal cutlets, round steaks, pounded
1½ cups bread crumbs
⅓ cup dried parmesan cheese
Egg wash (2 eggs, beaten lightly with ¼ cup milk)
4 Tablespoons butter
Small clove of garlic, minced
½ teaspoon salt
½ teaspoon coarsely ground pepper
½ teaspoon chopped basil
½ teaspoon chopped chervil
2 Tablespoons lemon juice
½ cup white wine
Lemon slices
Capers

WIENER SCHNITZEL

I can't recall a good Wiener Schnitzel ever being turned down, but tender it must be.

Flour the veal by putting the flour in a flat dinner plate and patting both sides of the veal into the flour. Melt the butter in a heavy skillet and add the veal. Lightly salt and pepper one side and fry until golden brown on both sides. This should take only a few minutes. Fry only as many pieces of veal at one time as you can get in the pan without crowding.

2 pounds veal scallops, cut from leg, sliced ¼" thick
Flour
Butter for frying
Salt
Freshly ground pepper

7
VEGETABLES & SALADS

VEGETABLES & SALADS

The sight of picture-perfect produce, dewy fresh and newly harvested from Lancaster County's patchwork of fertile fields, could inspire a still-life artist, for it certainly inspires cooks.

During our growing season, the list of crops coming in from the garden reads like a seed catalog's entire table of contents — from asparagus, Brussels sprouts and cabbage to eggplant, lima beans, rutabaga and salsify.

Although visitors could get into trouble if they began peering into backyard "patches" to see what's growing, our farmers' markets welcome those who seek a feast for the eye.

The aisles are lined with heads of cauliflower as big as basketballs. Tomatoes that outweigh softballs, bunches of celery so crisp that the crunch can be heard across the room and mushrooms whose snowy white caps could hide the Mad Hatter are all awaiting produce lovers who venture into this veritable Wonderland.

As you'll see, we make the most of some of our best-known products like root vegetables, mushrooms, cabbages and potatoes. Whatever you do, try my son Charlie's light and creamy potato salad if you want to know just how good potatoes can be.

Although I didn't know it when I was growing up, I guess we were vegetable pioneers. We ate sugar and snow peas long before they became universal ingredients in America's versions of Chinese stir-frys. We valued freshness. Tender spears of asparagus were picked twice a day to assure the greatest number of tips. (Even though I loved the taste, I despised the task. As the member of the family who stood closest to the ground, this elfin responsibility was all mine.) And four decades before West Coast chefs "discovered" miniature vegetables, my mother was using everything from baby carrots to baby gherkins.

I particularly remember the baby gherkins, picked just a day or two after the vines finished their blossom stage. Mother always added the baby gherkins to the special chow-chow (a sweet-and-sour vegetable relish) that was saved for entertaining guests. I'll never forget being smacked for picking some of those pickled baby gherkins out of the chow-chow before company arrived. I thought I had carefully rearranged the dish so no one would miss a few little gherkins, but my skill was no match for my mother's trained eye.

We certainly weren't pioneers when it came to our early vegetable cooking techniques, however. Overcooked vegetables have been a fact of life in our part of the country for years. Spinach was always cooked to mush and even when we had leafy

greens for salads, we drenched them with heavy dressings that made them wilt on the spot.

Today, I steam or stir-fry snow peas for just a minute or two so they retain much of their crunch and all of their flavor and color. When mother made them, she cooked them first in water, then in butter and cream and finally, poured them over patty shells. Sweet potatoes aren't just candied. They're simply baked or are grated and turned into pancakes.

Although I've forsaken the old ways (except when I'm cooking for my older relatives who say I'd be a good cook if only I'd learn to prepare vegetables properly), there are a few ideas I won't give up. My mashed potatoes will always be fluffy and real and they'll always contain a bit of canned, evaporated milk to make them extra fluffy and give them a depth of flavor you won't get any other way. I just can't help using a small amount of browned butter on vegetables and potatoes, for goodness sake.

Using browned butter, a Pennsylvania Dutch tradition, requires close attention. Focus your eyes and ears on the butter while it's cooking and it will tell you as soon as it is ready. When the hot butter foams up in the saucepan, it will be noisy. When the foam subsides and the butter quiets down, take it off the stove. Don't hesitate for a minute or you'll learn quickly that the difference between browned butter and burned butter is only a second or two.

Will there always be a place for browned butter in these days of health-conscious dining? There's value in it for almost everyone, with the exception of those on very strict diets, for as thrifty Pennsyvlanians long ago realized, browning provides a maximum of flavor from a minimum of butter.

MARINATED VEGETABLES

I had many requests for this recipe after my PM Magazine segment on gardening. Try any combination of your favorite vegetables on one of your prettiest platters. It will be a colorful addition to your next summer party.

Clean and slice the vegetables. If broccoli is used, cut the stem into strips and put in a pan with salted water to cover. Cook only until tender crisp, do not overcook. Remove the vegetables with tongs and drain on paper towels. In a small bowl, combine the lemon juice, garlic, oil, herbs, salt and pepper. Pour over the vegetables. Sprinkle with lemon zest, if desired. Cover with plastic wrap and refrigerate until cold. Drain with tongs or serve in marinade.

MARINADE

Juice of 2 lemons

4 cloves of garlic, cut into very thin slices

¾ cup olive oil

½ teaspoon oregano

½ teaspoon chives

½ teaspoon sweet basil

½ teaspoon mint leaves

Freshly ground black pepper to taste

VEGETABLES

Whole spring onions or slices of onion

Tomatoes, sliced

Zucchini, sliced

Yellow squash, sliced

Asparagus

Broccoli

1 Tablespoon finely grated lemon zest, yellow part only (optional)

Salt to taste (optional)

BUTTERED BEETS

You can't beat beets for color, flavor and nutrition, and even the greens can be used if they are young and fresh.

Remove tops and scrub beets. Place in saucepan and add salt and water. Cook until tender, approximately 30 minutes for medium sized beets. Save ½ cup juice. Run cold water over beets and remove skin, tails and tops. If beets are large, slice, grate or quarter. In saucepan blend butter, rind, juice, honey and cornstarch to beet juice and bring to boil. Add beets and simmer for 15 minutes. Check for seasonings, adding more salt if desired. Serve with a dot of butter on top.

1 pound beets, scrubbed
1 quart water
3 Tablespoons butter
1 Tablespoon grated orange rind
¼ cup orange juice
1 Tablespoon honey
1 Tablespoon cornstarch
½ teaspoon salt (optional)

BAKED CORN PUDDING

We always creamed the corn that was a bit too old to serve on the cob. When we had all we needed for the winter, we dried the rest for use in creamed dried corn and dried corn pudding. The flavors are very different, each wonderful.

Place all the ingredients in a food processor and blend, chopping the corn kernels and mixing thoroughly. If using frozen corn, place all the ingredients but the corn into the food processor, gradually adding the corn as it mixes. This prevents the motor from burning out. Pour into buttered 1½ quart baking dish and bake in a preheated 350° F. oven for 45 minutes. Top with chopped parsley or sprig of fresh basil.

MICROWAVE: Cook in a covered baking dish using waxed paper to cover for 15 minutes or until the egg mixture is set and firm. Let stand 3 to 5 minutes before serving.

3 cups fresh or frozen corn, cut off the cob
½ teaspoon salt
½ teaspoon white pepper
1½ Tablespoons flour
2½ Tablespoons melted butter
3 eggs, beaten
1 cup milk
½ teaspoon basil, chopped
1 teaspoon sugar (optional)

CORN AND SPINACH CASSEROLE

Butter an 8″ square cake pan or 1½ quart casserole. Sprinkle chopped onion in the pan. Add corn kernels. Sprinkle with ½ teaspoon salt and dash of pepper. Mix eggs with the milk and pour over the corn. In a bowl, add vinegar, salt and pepper to chopped spinach and toss until well seasoned. Place spinach mixture on top of corn. Sprinkle with cheese. Cover with bacon slices. Top with bread crumbs and bake in a preheated 375° F. oven for 45 minutes. Excellent served with roast veal, pork, pheasant or chicken.

MICROWAVE: Cook, covered, in your MICROWAVE for 15 minutes. Let stand 3 to 5 minutes before serving.

¼ cup onion, chopped
1 Tablespoon butter
3 cups fresh or frozen corn kernels
2 eggs, beaten
½ cup milk
1 teaspoon salt
¼ teaspoon freshly ground pepper
1 Tablespoon white wine vinegar
½ pound fresh spinach, coarsely chopped
2 Tablespoons grated parmesan cheese
¼ pound bacon slices
¼ cup dried bread crumbs

BAKED CORN SUPREME

So many folks ask me how to use dried corn. We developed this recipe for the John F. Cope Co. for their new dried corn package.

MICROWAVE: Grind the dried corn in a blender or food processor. Place in a buttered 2 quart casserole. Blend the milk, butter, eggs and salt. Pour over corn and mix thoroughly. Cover with wax paper. Cook on high for 12 minutes. Stir and complete cooking for 12 to 15 minutes. Let stand for 5 minutes before serving.

7.5 ounces dried sweet corn
3½ cups milk
3½ Tablespoons melted butter or margarine
4 eggs, lightly beaten
1 teaspoon salt (optional)

CREAMED DRIED CORN

Here's another great way to serve dried corn.

MICROWAVE: Place all the above ingredients in a buttered 2 quart casserole and mix thoroughly. Cover with wax paper and cook on high for 10 minutes. Stir and let stand for 15 minutes. Complete cooking for 15 minutes.

7.5 ounces dried sweet corn
3½ cups milk
2 Tablespoons butter or margarine
¼ teaspoon salt (optional)

SPINACH CHEESE SQUARES

Melt the butter in a 9″ x 12″ pan in the oven. Beat eggs, add flour, salt, pepper, milk and baking powder. Add cheeses, and spinach and mix well. Pour into the prepared pan and sprinkle with nutmeg and the crumbled bacon. Bake in a preheated 350° F. oven for 35 minutes. Cool a half hour before serving and cut into squares. This freezes well.

¼ cup butter
3 eggs
1 cup flour
1 cup milk
1½ teaspoons salt
Freshly ground pepper
1 teaspoon baking powder
1 pound grated white cheese, ½ sharp cheddar and ½ mild cheddar
4 cups fresh spinach, chopped
Sprinkle of nutmeg
½ pound bacon, cooked and crumbled for top

CUCUMBER SALAD

Peel cucumbers and slice thin. Place in a large bowl and add onion if desired. Sprinkle with salt. Place a saucer or small plate on top of the cucumbers and press with a heavy weight for several hours. I use a #10 can. Drain the liquid well. Combine the vinegar, sugar, pepper and sour cream, mix well, and pour over the cucumbers. Blend thoroughly and chill before serving.

3 medium cucumbers
1 teaspoon salt
4 Tablespoons cider vinegar
½ cup sugar
¼ teaspoon pepper
¾ cup sour cream
1 small onion, finely cut (optional)

FROZEN PICKLES

Mix cucumbers, onions and salt together and let stand for 2 hours. Drain and rinse well with fresh water to remove the salt. Mix the sugar, vinegar and dill weed together and pour over the cucumbers and onions. Let stand, stirring occasionally, until the sugar is dissolved and the liquid covers all. Pack into 2 pint jars and freeze.

4 cups cucumbers, thinly sliced
2 cups onions, thinly sliced
4 Tablespoons salt
2 Tablespoons water
¾ cup sugar
½ cup cider vinegar
1 teaspoon dill weed

MELISSA'S CANDIED BAKED BEANS

Melissa Herman wrote our story that appeared in PEOPLE Magazine.

Soak beans in water overnight. Cook until soft but not mushy, about 30 to 40 minutes. Brown bacon in skillet, remove and drain on paper towels. Break into bite-sized pieces. Sauté the onions in bacon fat for approximately 5 minutes. Combine beans, sugar, bacon and onion in 3 quart baking dish. Add enough water to have beans covered. Bake in a preheated 300° F. oven for 5 hours, adding water as necessary to keep beans from drying out.

1 pound Great Northern dried beans
1 pound granulated sugar
½ pound bacon
1 cup chopped onion

BAKED CABBAGE

Cut cabbage in wedges ¼″ thick and boil in water for 10 minutes. Drain well and place in a buttered casserole. Sprinkle with the flour, salt, pepper, chives, chervil and sugar. Dot with butter. Pour the hot milk over the cabbage and top with the grated cheese.
Bake in a preheated 350° F. oven for 35 minutes.

1 medium head cabbage
2 Tablespoons flour
1 teaspoon salt
Freshly ground pepper
½ teaspoon chives
1 teaspoon chervil
2 Tablespoons sugar
3 Tablespoons butter
1 cup hot milk
½ cup grated cheese

BAKED SAUERKRAUT

Put the sauerkraut in a greased 1½ quart casserole, add the prunes, currants, sugar and nutmeg, and mix well. Bake in a pre-heated 350° F. oven for 45 to 55 minutes until golden brown. Stir frequently to make sure that the sauerkraut browns evenly.

VARIATION

Add smoked meats or precooked pork spareribs or pork chops during the baking.

4 cups loosely packed fresh or canned sauerkraut
1 cup prunes, pitted
½ cup currants or white raisins
¼ cup light brown sugar
¼ teaspoon freshly grated nutmeg

DUTCH HOT SLAW

Shred the cabbage in a food processor and add to 1″ to 2″ of water in a saucepan. Cover and cook until tender, 5 to 8 minutes. Drain and keep hot. Beat together all the rest of the ingredients except the cream or milk. Melt butter in a medium saucepan and add the mixture. Cook until thickened, stirring constantly. Remove from the heat and add the cream or milk. Beat until smooth and pour over the hot cabbage.

6 cups cabbage, shredded
2 eggs, beaten lightly
1½ teaspoons sugar
¼ cup vinegar
¼ cup water
¼ cup cream or milk
1 Tablespoon butter
½ teaspoon dry mustard
½ teaspoon salt
⅛ teaspoon paprika

DANDELION SALAD WITH HOT BACON DRESSING

In colonial days as well as now, some things must be enjoyed for a very short time. Each year when the new dandelion stalks appear, this salad is the best "spring tonic" one may enjoy. It is rich in iron and more tasty than endive or the more ordinary greens. The stalk must be picked before the blossoms appear.

Wash the greens thoroughly and place in large or individual bowls. Fry the bacon in a skillet or microwave oven until crisp. Remove and drain on paper towels, crumbling or breaking into bits. Top greens with sliced hard boiled eggs. Pour the Hot Bacon Dressing over the salad and top with chopped chives and bacon. Serve immediately.

VARIATION

Any tender garden greens or spinach may be substituted.

6 cups loosely packed young
  dandelion greens, washed
  and cleaned
4 slices bacon
4 eggs, hard boiled and peeled
1 Tablespoon chives, chopped
Hot Bacon Dressing

HOT BACON DRESSING

In a deep skillet, fry the bacon until crisp. Remove and drain on paper towels. In a small bowl, combine the cornstarch, salt and sugar. Add the eggs, stirring with a whisk until smooth, then slowly add the vinegar. Blend milk with egg mixture and slowly add to the bacon fat in the skillet. Return skillet to the stove and place on low to medium heat, stirring constantly. Bring to a boil and continue to boil for 1 minute, stirring continually with whisk. Break the bacon into bits and add half of the bacon to the dressing. Save the rest for garnishing salads.

This dressing may be served cold, but it is tastier when hot or warm. It reheats nicely in a MICROWAVE oven.

½ pound bacon
2 Tablespoons cornstarch
1½ teaspoons salt
3 Tablespoons granulated
  sugar
2 eggs, slightly beaten
⅓ cup cider vinegar
2 cups milk

MUSHROOM BUSINESS

Slice the mushrooms and sauté them in butter in a large skillet. Remove from heat and add the celery, green pepper, onions, mayonnaise, salt and pepper. Place 3 slices of buttered and cubed bread into a 2 quart buttered casserole. Cover with the mushroom mixture. On top of this, place 3 more slices of buttered, cubed bread. Pour the beaten eggs and milk, whipped together, over all. Spread the soup on top and cover with the last 2 slices of buttered bread cubes. Bake in a preheated 325° F. oven for 50 to 60 minutes. Sprinkle with the shredded cheese during the last 10 minutes of cooking time.

1 **pound mushrooms**
2 **Tablespoons butter**
½ **cup celery, chopped**
½ **cup green pepper, chopped**
½ **cup onion, chopped**
½ **cup mayonnaise**
¾ **teaspoon salt**
¼ **teaspoon pepper**
8 **slices buttered bread, cut in cubes**
2 **eggs, lightly beaten**
1½ **cups milk**
1¼ **cups mushroom soup, concentrated**
½ **cup American cheese, shredded**

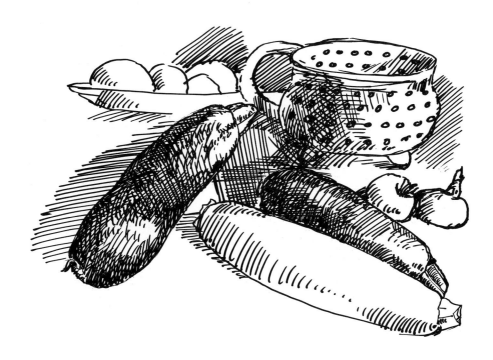

TURKEY-MUSHROOM SALAD

Combine the turkey, mushrooms, celery and olives; toss lightly. Blend the mayonnaise, lemon juice, onion, salt, pepper and parsley together and add to the turkey mixture. Chill thoroughly before serving.

2½ cups cooked turkey, cubed

1½ cups mushrooms, sliced

1 cup celery, chopped

⅓ cup large, stuffed green olives, sliced

⅓ cup mayonnaise or salad dressing

1 Tablespoon lemon juice

1 teaspoon onion, finely chopped

½ teaspoon salt

Freshly ground pepper

¼ cup fresh parsley, finely chopped (optional)

CREAMED MUSHROOMS

Sauté mushrooms, pepper and chervil in the butter until lightly browned and most of the liquid has evaporated. Stir in the cream and mix well. Cook another minute or so until heated thoroughly. If the sauce seems too thick, thin with a splash of white wine. Spoon over the pastry squares or toast and sprinkle with paprika.

3 cups mushrooms, sliced

¼ teaspoon freshly ground pepper

◆ Pinch chervil

3 Tablespoons butter

⅓ cup light cream or half-and-half

◆ Sprinkle of paprika

Pastry Squares or toast

RUBY'S GREEN BEANS

These are quick and easy to make, but a little different than usual. You can use fresh, canned or frozen beans. My family likes the canned best because of their flavor.

Put the drained beans in a saucepan and add the rest of the ingredients. Toss lightly without cutting into the beans and heat thoroughly. Cover and turn the heat to warm to allow the seasonings to go into the beans. Taste and add salt and pepper if desired.

- 2 15½ ounce cans cut, green beans, drained
- 1 Tablespoon butter
- ½ teaspoon dry mustard
- ◆ Dash of onion powder
- ◆ Dash of garlic powder

PEA AND PEANUT SALAD

Combine the sour cream, mayonnaise, worcestershire sauce, salt, dill weed and curry powder. Drain peas and corn and mix them with the peanuts. Pour the sour cream mixture over the peas, corn and nuts and mix. Serve cold. It's even better the next day.

- ½ cup sour cream onion dip
- 1 Tablespoon mayonnaise
- 1 teaspoon worcestershire sauce
- 1 teaspoon salt
- ½ teaspoon dried dill weed
- ¼ teaspoon curry powder
- 1 10 ounce package frozen peas, thawed but not cooked
- ¾ cup whole kernel corn
- 2 Tablespoons pimento, chopped
- ⅔ cup dry roasted peanuts without hulls

MASHED POTATOES

Evaporated milk keeps potatoes fluffy and helps retain the heat. Important tip — do not use newly dug red or white potatoes.

Place peeled and quartered potatoes in large kettle with salt and water. Boil for approximately 35 minutes until soft. Remove with slotted spoon and place in large mixing bowl. Mix on slow speed, slowly adding the evaporated milk, heated milk and butter. Whip until very fluffy. Serve in heated bowl and top with Browned Butter.

1½ **pounds white potatoes, peeled and quartered (Kennebec, Idaho or Irish Cobbler are best)**

1 **teaspoon salt**

1 **quart water**

⅓ **cup evaporated milk**

⅓ **cup milk, heated**

4 to 6 **Tablespoons butter**

½ **teaspoon freshly ground pepper**

Browned Butter for topping, see Index

HOME FRIED POTATOES

This old-fashioned dish is never out of style. Brown outside, but tender inside, these could be a meal for folks like me who love potatoes with a passion.

Scrub potatoes, peel (some prefer to let the skins on) and slice very thin. A food processor slices these as quick as a wink. In a large skillet or fry pan brown the bacon, saving the fat for frying the potatoes. Place bacon on paper towels, crumbling into pieces. Add the potatoes, pepper, onion and chives and brown, turning often to prevent burning. After 5 minutes, add the water and cover skillet, reducing heat to medium. When brown on each side and soft in the middle, top with bacon pieces and serve immediately.

1½ **pounds white potatoes, peeled and sliced thin**

6 **slices bacon**

½ **teaspoon coarsely ground pepper**

½ **cup onion, chopped (optional)**

1 **Tablespoon chives, chopped**

⅓ **cup water**

BAKED POTATOES

Choose a variety of baking potato that is fresh, not wrinkled with sprouts, and make sure that they are all the same size. This saves time and insures uniform cooking in the MICROWAVE or oven.

Scrub potatoes thoroughly and prick the skin twice to keep the skin from exploding in the oven. If you prefer the skin soft, rub with vegetable oil or salad dressing. Place the potatoes in shallow baking pan and bake in preheated 400° F. oven for 1 hour or until soft when squeezed gently with a pot holder. Serve immediately, cutting a cross in the middle and squeezing both ends together to let the fluffy potato pop through.

VARIATION

Sweet Potatoes, baked whole or sliced in half lengthwise, are excellent, but reduce baking time by 15 minutes. Follow directions for Baked Potatoes.

MICROWAVE : Place potatoes on paper towel in a circle, leaving 1 inch between each, and prick the skins with a fork. Each medium size potato takes approximately 4 minutes on high. Halfway through the cooking time, turn them over. Let stand for 10 minutes, covered with clean towel, until ready to serve.

1 potato per person
Butter, salt and pepper
Serve with all your favorites like cheese, parsley, sautéed mushrooms, sour cream and chives, minced ham, crumbled bacon, herb cheese and bologna-cheese spread.

POTATO SALAD

Guests at Groff's Farm have asked for this recipe for years. Charlie has finally consented to printing his specialty. Bravo! It's definitely his claim to fame!!

Peel and cook the potatoes until medium soft; then drain, slice and cool. Mix the mayonnaise and sour cream together, then add all the rest of the ingredients. Let the salad stand for at least 3 hours, overnight if possible. This recipe can be cut in half for a smaller number of servings.

- 4 cups heavy mayonnaise
- 2 cups sour cream
- ½ cup apple cider vinegar
- 1 cup granulated sugar
- ½ Tablespoon white pepper
- 2 Tablespoons dry mustard
- ¼ cup celery seed
- 2 Tablespoons worcestershire sauce
- 2 Tablespoons lemon juice
- ½ cup fresh parsley, chopped
- 2 Tablespoons chives, chopped
- 1 cup onion, minced
- 1 cup celery, minced
- 10 pounds potatoes, preferably new if possible
- ¼ cup salt

CANDIED YAMS WITH PECANS

Either boil the yams in their jackets until soft, or cook in the MICROWAVE. If using the MICROWAVE, scrub the yams and pierce each one with a fork several times and cook on full power for 8 to 12 minutes, then let stand for 5 more minutes. Let cool, peel, and slice. Place half of the slices in a buttered casserole and cover with half of the sugar, molasses, butter, vanilla and pecans, then do the same thing with the other half of the yams. Bake uncovered for 45 minutes or longer in a preheated 350° F. oven.

- 6 medium yams, 6 to 8 ounces each
- ½ cup brown sugar
- ½ cup golden molasses
- 4 Tablespoons butter
- 2 teaspoons vanilla
- 1 to 1½ cups pecans

SWEET POTATO PANCAKES WITH PINEAPPLE SAUCE

Peel the sweet potatoes and grate in a food processor (makes about 4 cups, loosely packed) or by hand. Mix the salt and flour together and toss with the grated potatoes. Lightly beat the eggs with a fork and add to the mixture , stirring well. Melt the shortening in a deep skillet and drop the batter, by spoonful, into the hot oil. Fry on each side until golden brown. Drain on paper towels. Serve with Pineapple Sauce, see below.

6 medium sweet potatoes
⅓ cup flour
1 teaspoon salt, less if desired
3 eggs
½ cup shortening

PINEAPPLE SAUCE

Delicious served with Sweet Potato Pancakes

Mix the cinnamon, nutmeg, and cornstarch in ¼ cup of the pineapple juice, stirring to remove any lumps. Heat the rest of the juice and stir the mixture into the hot liquid to thicken it. Add the brown sugar, then the crushed fruit. Serve when heated thoroughly.

1 cup pineapple juice
½ teaspoon cinnamon
½ teaspoon nutmeg
2 Tablespoons cornstarch
2 Tablespoons brown sugar
1 cup crushed pineapple

ACORN SQUASH WITH HAMBURG STUFFING

A pretty Entrée for a Fall or Winter luncheon.

Wash and cut each squash in half and scoop out the seeds. Trim the little point off the bottoms so they will stand straight while cooking. Melt 2 Tablespoons of butter and brush the inside of each cup. Sprinkle with a little salt and place the 6 servings in a baking dish. Add water half-way up the dish and bake in a preheated 375° F. oven for 45 minutes. Melt the other 2 Tablespoons of butter in a skillet and brown the onion. Add the meat and stir to break it up while it's cooking. Don't overcook since it will be cooked more. Drain and stir in the salt, lemon pepper and chervil. Put ¼ cup of the hamburg mixture into each squash cup and continue baking for another 15 to 20 minutes. Top with the crabapple jelly, a heaping teaspoon on each, for the last 15 minutes.

- 3 acorn squash
- 4 Tablespoons butter
- 1½ pounds ground chuck
- 3 Tablespoons onion, chopped
- ½ teaspoon salt
- ½ teaspoon lemon pepper
- 1 teaspoon chervil
- ⅓ cup crabapple jelly

BAKED SALSIFY

Mother Groff served salsify in the same recipes that required oysters. With nine children to feed, oysters were out of the question. Many children learn to love oysters for the same reason, — the mild flavor with a hint of the sea.

Wash and scrape the salsify and cook in salted water (½ teaspoon if desired) until tender, approximately 15 minutes, depending on the thickness of the vegetable. Slice ½″ thick. Line a buttered casserole with half the salsify, crackers, pepper and butter. Add the rest of the salsify, crackers, pepper and all the milk. Top with remaining butter and bake in preheated 375° F. oven for 35 minutes.

Serves 4

1   pound salsify
2   cups small oyster crackers (broken saltines may be substituted)
½   teaspoon coarsely ground pepper
¼   cup melted butter
1½ cups milk or half-and-half

SAUTEED APPLE-MINT SLICES

Goes well with lamb chops.

Core and slice the apples. Do not peel. Combine the butter, lemon juice, sugar, syrup and jelly and mix well. Place the apple slices in a shallow baking dish and brush them with the mixture. Bake in a preheated 350° F. oven for 15 minutes until glazed and bubbling.

2   apples, cored and sliced
1   Tablespoon butter, melted
1   teaspoon lemon juice
1   Tablespoon brown sugar
2   teaspoons corn syrup
2   Tablespoons mint jelly

APRICOT CHEESE DELIGHT

Drain the fruits and reserve the juices. Chill the fruit. Dissolve the gelatin in boiling water and add 1 cup of the reserved juice. Chill until slightly thickened. Fold in fruit and marshmallows. Pour into cold, water-rinsed 9" x 11" x 2" dish and chill. Combine sugar and flour and blend in the beaten egg. Gradually stir in the juice. Cook over low heat until thickened, stirring constantly. Remove from heat. Stir in the butter and cool. Fold in whipped cream and spread over chilled gelatin mixture. Sprinkle top with grated cheese and chill. To serve, arrange squares of salad on lettuce.

Makes 12 servings

BOTTOM LAYER

- 1 can (29 ounces) apricots, drained and cut fine
- 1 can (29 ounces) crushed pineapple, drained
- 2 packages orange-flavored gelatin
- 2 cups hot water
- 1 cup combined apricot and pineapple juice
- ¾ cup miniature marshmallows

TOPPING

- ½ cup sugar
- 3 Tablespoons all-purpose flour
- 1 egg, slightly beaten
- 1 cup combined pineapple and apricot juice
- 2 Tablespoons butter
- 1 cup whipping cream, whipped
- ¾ cup cheddar cheese, grated

POPPY SEED DRESSING

This is the House Dressing at the Cameron Estate Inn.

Put all of the ingredients in a blender and mix well. Serve on a mixed green salad or with fruit. Keeps well.

- 1½ cups vegetable oil
- ½ cup cider vinegar
- Salt and pepper to taste
- ◆ Scant cup of granulated sugar
- ¼ cup onion, chopped
- 1½ Tablespoons poppy seeds

PRETZEL SALAD

Mix the pretzels, butter and 1 Tablespoon of the sugar together and press into the bottom of a 9″ x 12″ baking dish or pan and bake in a preheated 400° F. oven for 8 minutes. Cool. Mix the cream cheese, 1 cup of sugar and topping together and spread them on the cooled crust. Dissolve the jello in the boiling water and add the strawberries. Pour the mixture over the cheese layer and chill until firm.

2 cups pretzels, crushed

¾ cup butter or margarine, melted

1 cup, plus 1 Tablespoon sugar

8 ounces cream cheese

~~1 cup sugar~~

2 cups of frozen non-dairy topping

2 small boxes, 3 ounces each, strawberry jello

2 cups boiling water

2 10 ounce packages frozen strawberries.

AVOCADO DELUXE SALAD

To the avocado and banana, add the lime and lemon juice to prevent browning. Sprinkle with the cardamon and add the apples, grapes, dates, nuts, coconut and the nutmeg. Toss lightly and serve in a crystal bowl with a larger bowl of crushed ice underneath.

- 3 avocados, peeled and cut in cubes
- 2 bananas, sliced
- ◆ Juice of 1 lime
- ◆ Juice of 1 lemon
- ¼ teaspoon cardamon
- 2 apples, cut in cubes
- 1 cup seedless grapes
- ½ cup dates, pitted and chopped
- 1 cup pecans or walnuts, broken and coarsely chopped
- ½ cup fresh coconut, grated or in small chunks
- ◆ Dash of nutmeg

Sprigs of fresh mint for garnish (optional)

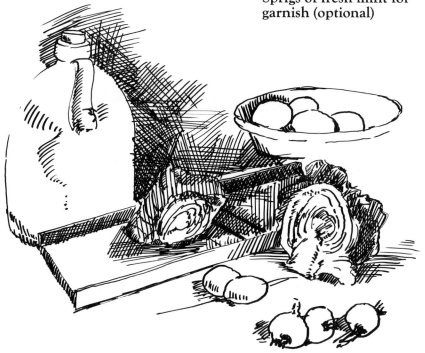

"EGG"CITING SPINACH SALAD

Wash spinach thoroughly and remove any large stems and drain. Wash lettuce, drain and mix with spinach. Slice onion and separate into rings. Wipe mushrooms with paper towel and slice ¼" thick. Core and slice the apples. Cut the hard boiled eggs in quarters. Toss or arrange salad to your liking and arrange the eggs around the edges. Pour a bit of the dressing over the salad and serve extra dressing on the side.

8 ounces young spinach
4 ounces spring cutting lettuce
1 red onion
4 ounces fresh mushrooms
2 red apples
4 hard boiled eggs, peeled
Creamy sweet and sour dressing, see Index

PINEAPPLE WITH RASPBERRY SAUCE

This can be served as a salad or dessert.

To cut the pineapple, use a very sharp knife to cut in half lengthwise, cutting all the way through the leaves. Cut the halves in half and remove the core in the center of each wedge. Use a grapefruit knife to cut the meat from the shell. Save the shells for serving. Cut the fruit in bite size pieces and place in shells, leaving the good leaves on for decoration. Place filled shells on salad plates garnished with a leaf of fresh lettuce and a flower. Serve the raspberry sauce on the side in a pretty glass pitcher or bowl.

Pineapple shells may be frozen and used later.

1 ripe pineapple
Lettuce
Fresh flowers for garnish
Raspberry sauce, see below

RASPBERRY SAUCE

In a small saucepan blend water and cornstarch. Stir in the berries and cook until thickened. Press through a sieve. If using brandy, heat the brandy and add to the warm sauce when ready to serve. Ignite the brandy at the table. Pour sauce over the fruit.

¼ cup water
1 Tablespoon cornstarch
10 ounces frozen red raspberries, thawed
¼ cup brandy, (optional)

FRESH FRUIT SALAD WITH POPPY SEED DRESSING

Light and refreshing, this is a perfect summer salad.

Wash all the fruit. Peel the melons and apples if you like, but there is more color if you leave them on. Slice the fruit into desired thickness. Break the grapes into small bunches. Peel the kiwi fruit and slice about ¼" thick. Place leaf of lettuce on each salad plate and arrange fruit for best eye appeal and color combination. Pour a small amount of poppy seed dressing over the fruit and serve extra dressing on the side.

All fresh fruits are wonderful, so use your imagination.

½ melon
½ honeydew melon
2 cups watermelon balls
2 apples, cored
Seedless grapes, several small
    bunches
2 Kiwi fruit
Lettuce
Poppy seed dressing, see Index

BAKED APPLES, EXTRAORDINARY

These apples are great instead of a green salad when served with pork dishes.

Blend flour, brown sugar, cinnamon, nutmeg and butter in food processor until crumbly. Core and peel apples. With a fork, scratch the sides of the apples on all sides and roll in the crumb mixture, packing as much as possible on the sides. Place the apples in a greased baking dish. Combine the granulated sugar, nuts and jam. Spoon into the cavities of apples. Bake in preheated 350° F. oven for 45 minutes or until apples are tender and crisp. Serve warm with whipped cream.

- 1 cup flour
- 1 cup light brown sugar
- 1 teaspoon cinnamon
- ¼ teaspoon nutmeg
- ½ cup butter or margarine
- 6 baking apples
- ¼ cup granulated sugar
- ⅓ cup chopped cashews or pecans
- ¼ cup currant jam or cranberry jelly
- Whipped cream

APPLE BUTTER

The wonderful aroma while making this Apple Butter will bring back memories of years gone by. The flavor is the same, with much less work.

Cook the apples and water in a pan over low heat until soft, about 20 minutes. Rub through a food mill.

Add the sugar, cider vinegar, and cinnamon, mixing well. Put mixture in a heavy roaster pan, uncovered, and cook in a preheated 375° F. oven for approximately 2½ hours, stirring every 15 minutes with a wooden spoon. The apple butter is thick enough when you can put 2 Tablespoons of the mixture on a saucer and turn it upside down without its dropping off.

Ladle into hot sterilized pint or quart jars and seal. Makes about 3½ quarts, or 7 pints.

- 12 pounds tart cooking apples, peeled, cored, and quartered (in the Fall use Winesap apples)
- 2 cups water
- 3½ cups granulated sugar
- 1 cup cider vinegar
- 1 teaspoon cinnamon

CREAMY SWEET-SOUR DRESSING

Blend the vinegar, sugar, milk, salt, pepper, celery seed and herbs in a small bowl until all the sugar is dissolved. Cover and refrigerate for 30 minutes.

½ cup cider vinegar or wine vinegar

⅔ cup sugar

¾ cup evaporated milk

½ teaspoon salt

◆ Several dashes freshly ground pepper

½ teaspoon celery seed

1 Tablespoon chopped fresh herbs, thyme, rosemary, chives, etc.

WHITE SAUCES

In a 1 quart saucepan, heat the shortening. Gradually add flour, stirring with whisk, until it becomes a smooth paste. Gradually add the milk, stirring constantly, until thickened. Add salt and pepper and reduce heat to very low. Stir for at least a minute before adding to prepared dish.

THIN
- 1 Tablespoon shortening
- 1 Tablespoon flour
- 1 cup milk
- ¼ teaspoon salt
- ◆ Dash freshly ground pepper

MEDIUM
- 2 Tablespoons shortening
- 2 Tablespoons flour
- 1 cup milk
- ¼ teaspoon salt
- ◆ Dash freshly ground pepper

THICK
- 3 Tablespoons shortening
- 3 Tablespoons flour
- 1 cup milk
- ¼ teaspoon salt
- ◆ Dash freshly ground pepper

ROUX

A shortening and flour mixture which is the basis of all white, blond or brown flour sauces. The amount of shortening is generally slightly more than that of flour. To prepare, melt shortening, stir in flour (off heat) and pour in water, stock or milk. Simmer until thickened.

HOLLANDAISE SAUCE

In mixing bowl or top of double boiler, add egg yolks and wine, beating thoroughly. If not using a double boiler, place bowl in pan of boiling water. Be careful not to cook the yolks — just heat them — always beating with wire wisk. When egg yolks are warm, slowly add clarified butter, mixing all the time until smooth and thickened. Gradually mix in the lemon juice, tabasco, salt and pepper. Keep warm, not hot, or it will break (curdle). If it breaks, add another egg yolk and beat vigorously.

2 egg yolks
1 Tablespoon white wine
½ cup Clarified Butter
2 drops tabasco
Juice of ½ lemon
Salt and white pepper to taste

CLARIFIED BUTTER

Place butter in deep sauce pan and cook on medium heat till it foams. Remove from heat and skim foam from top. The clear yellow liquid is the clarified butter. Do not use the solids and milky liquid on the bottom.

1 cup butter

BROWNED BUTTER

Melt ½ pound butter over medium-low heat in a heavy 1 quart saucepan (the butter has a tendency to boil over, so make sure you have a big enough pan). After it melts, stir occasionally until it starts to brown. Remove from heat before it burns. If it gets too dark, it will lose its flavor and become bitter; it should be just a rich nut brown.

COOKING METHODS FOR FRESH GARDEN VEGETABLES

ASPARAGUS

Tie 6 to 8 stalks in a bunch, and cook upright in a coffeepot or saucepan in several inches of salted water for about 8 minutes. Asparagus should not be overcooked or it will lose its beautiful bright green color and flavor. It can be cooked laying flat in a skillet in a small amount of salted water for 6 minutes. Serve with browned butter, Hollandaise, a squirt of fresh lemon juice or in a marinade. Asparagus is also good stir-fried, cut diagonally, until bright green and crispy tender.

GREEN OR YELLOW SNAP BEANS

Wash beans and remove the tips and strings by snapping or using a paring knife. Cook whole or cut in pieces in salted, boiling water for 15 minutes. They're good cooked in any broth or with your choice of seasoning added to the water. Serve with browned butter, add slivered almonds. or a sprinkle of nutmeg for variety. Some people like their beans cooked for a long time and some until just barely tender. I prefer the color, flavor and texture of crisp vegetables.

BROCCOLI

Remove large leaves and cut the stalk from the buds. Peel the stalk and cut into slices or julienne strips. Place in about an inch of salted, boiling water and cook for about 10 minutes. Don't overcook, it should be tender-crisp. Serve with browned butter, Hollandaise, marinated or with Cheese Sauce, see Index.

BRUSSELS SPROUTS

Wash thoroughly and trim the stem. Cook in an inch of salted, boiling water with a lid until just tender, about 8 to 10 minutes. Serve with browned butter, pecans, chestnuts or Cheese Sauce, see Index.

CARROTS

Scrape or pare very thinly and cut the way you prefer. Steam in a small amount of salted water until just tender or melt a little butter in a skillet and sauté. Cook, covered with a lid, for about 5 minutes. Stir several times during the cooking time. Season to taste. Carrots have such a sweet flavor that they only need browned butter to enhance them.

CAULIFLOWER

Wash thoroughly and remove the leaves and the core. Separate into flowerets or leave the head whole. I prefer to serve the whole head with Cheese Sauce. Cook in an inch of salted, boiling water until just tender, about 20 minutes. Check with a fork. Drain and serve with butter, cream, Hollandaise or just plain. Try cauliflower dipped in batter and deep fried or raw with a dip, see Index for batter.

PEAS AND SUGAR PEAS, *known to many folks as* SNOW PEAS

Shell and wash the peas. Cook, covered, in a small amount of salted, boiling water for 8 to 10 minutes, until just tender. You may prefer to include a pinch of sugar or a couple of pods while cooking for extra flavor. Drain, add salt, pepper and butter

to taste. Sugar peas are very delicate and don't need to be cooked very long. They can be steamed quickly by using 2 or 3 large lettuce leaves. Wash them and DON'T shake off the water. Lay them in the bottom of a saucepan, put the snapped, washed pods on top, cover with a lid and cook just until all of the water has evaporated. They should be crisp and bright green. Sugar peas are a nice addition to any stir-fry too.

POTATOES

New potatoes may be served scrubbed and cooked in a small amount of boiling water until just tender. I like to scrape them, which takes a lot more time than peeling, but the flavor is so much better. Topped with browned butter, folks will think there are secret spices added, but it's only the natural goodness coming through.

PARSNIPS, TURNIPS, KOHLRABI AND RUTABAGA

All of these vegetables retain their colors well when they are cooked, and are pleasing to the eye when peeled and sliced, diced or cubed. They're all cooked the same way, for about 20 to 25 minutes in boiling broth of any kind. Check for seasoning and add as desired, depending on the strength of the broth. Add butter if desired.

TOMATOES

Tomatoes are usually served fresh, stewed, broiled or fried. To stew, cook in a small amount of water, depending on your planned use for them, and when soft, add them to your stew, sauce or eat them plain with bread cubes. You may choose to add a little sugar and some salt and pepper. Broiled tomatoes are usually halved and dotted with a little butter, salt and pepper and sometimes cheese. You may add any herb then if desired. Broil until heated through and the butter or cheese is bubbly and slightly browned. To fry slices, choose a firm red or green tomato, dip it in seasoned flour and fry in a skillet in melted butter until golden brown on each side.

SUMMER SQUASH

Pattypan, zucchini, straightneck or yellow crookneck are all summer squash and I prefer to cook them with the skin, unpeeled. When peeled they lack color and become mushy quickly. To sauté, slice and lightly brown in a skillet with some butter and seasoning to taste. You may want to add chopped onion to the butter first for added flavor. To steam, cook in a small amount of boiling, salted water until tender, a very short time. Squash slices are very good deep fried in my Beer Batter, see Index. Tender squash can be halved and buttered, then sprinkled with crumbs, seasonings, chopped onion, tomato and shredded cheese and broiled until tender and the topping is lightly browned. Don't over-cook.

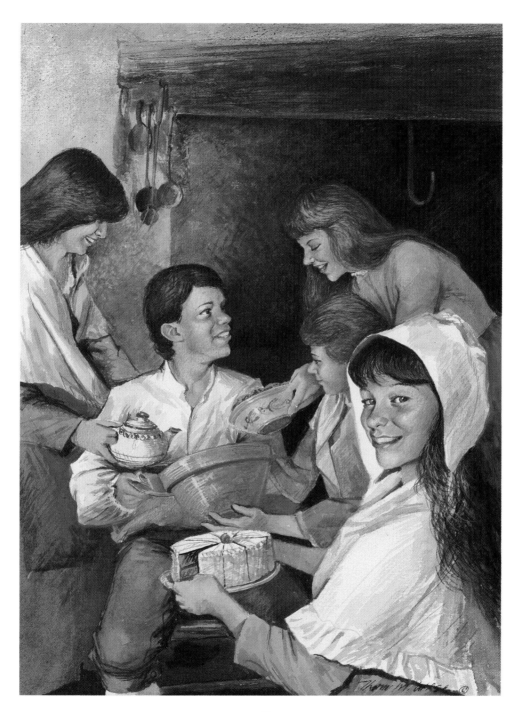

8

DESSERTS

DESSERTS

D on't venture into this chapter if you're trying to stay on a diet because your reserve will melt right along with the caramels that ooze into the nooks and crannies of the caramel apple pie!

No calories have been trimmed from the pies, cakes, puddings, frostings or special treats like cashew brittle because I have a reputation to uphold. My aunt, who was the family's pie baker, and my mother, who was in charge of yeast breads, cakes and candies, didn't believe in low-calorie creations. They pulled out all the stops because dessert time was a time for them to show their sparkle.

When our family was entertaining guests, dinner included both pies and cakes. Usually, a cake with pudding was dished up between the first and second servings of the main course and dessert for the meal was pie with ice cream. That was living!

When Abe and I were courting, my chocolate cake with caramel icing helped me win his heart and he has been my dessert critic ever since.

To this day, that chocolate cake and another childhood favorite of mine, cracker pudding, are given to guests at the Farm Restaurant at the start of the meal, rather than at the finish. Why? Because I want them to have a taste of these treats before they're too full to care.

The emphasis we place on desserts is in keeping with Pennsylvania tradition, for, it is said, that one can tell the time of day, time of year and even the occasion, by the pies brought to the table in Pennsylvania Dutch Country.

Ever since the early days, Pennsylvania cooks have put practically anything between two crusts, from green tomatoes to corn sliced fresh from the cob. For that matter, they've even managed to make something out of almost nothing by creating Johnny Pies. Simply scraps of dough pressed into tart pans and filled with little more than flour, sugar, cinnamon, milk and butter, these were special treats made for children. The filling is so thin that people who like them have been accused of eating pies with nothing in them.

Our area is known for such treats as Shoofly pie, Amish vanilla pie, and funny pie (a cross between a pie and cake with a gooey layer of chocolate serving as the dividing line). In the old days when people gathered for barn raisings, weddings, or other social events, it was no wonder they sometimes stacked all the pies in a mound, creating a "stack pie," and sliced down through the mound so everyone got a taste of each pie.

You're not going to want to do that with the new recipes we've cooked up. Taste the special and devilishly rich funny pie and chocolate walnut pie. Try the raspberry crumb pie and the cakes (including several of my mother's favorites) and you'll agree that each of these desserts is worth savoring on its own.

When you take the time to make one of the desserts, be sure there are no well-meaning food editors around.

To explain, I'll never forget the cooking class I gave that included delicate glazed strawberry tartlets. At the end of the class, I neatly placed some 30 of the tarts, topped with dollops of whipped cream, on a tray, so I could have my picture taken. Just before the newspaper photographer snapped the picture, the newspaper's food editor rushed in and bent over the work counter to remove some of the dishes and ingredients she didn't want in the photo. When she stood up, she bumped my tray and the tartlets went flying. I managed to catch half of them before the rest unceremoniously hit the carpet with gentle thuds. The picture was taken with the tarts that were left, and the food editor and I are still friends. After all, she certainly flipped over my desserts.

CHOCOLATE MOUSSE CAKE

There is no flour used in this cake.

Preheat oven to 325° F. Melt the chocolate and butter in a small saucepan over low heat, stirring so as not to scorch it. In a large bowl, beat the egg yolks and ¾ cup sugar until very light and fluffy, about 5 minutes. Gradually beat in warm chocolate mixture and vanilla. In another large bowl, beat egg whites with cream of tartar until soft peaks form. Add remaining ¼ cup sugar, one Tablespoon at a time. Continue beating until stiff. Fold egg whites into chocolate and mix. Pour ¾ of the batter into a 10″ ungreased springform pan. Cover remaining batter and refrigerate. Bake the cake for 35 minutes. Prepare the frosting and set aside. As the cake is cooling the center will drop. When it is cool, remove the outside ring of the springform pan. Stir the refrigerated batter to soften slightly. Spread on top of the cake. The batter fills in the cake where it has dropped. Refrigerate until firm. May be refrigerated overnight or placed in the freezer until ready to use. Spread frosting over the top and sides and garnish with cherries and chocolate.

7 ounces semi-sweet chocolate bits
¼ pound butter, unsalted
7 eggs, separated
1 cup sugar
1 teaspoon vanilla
⅛ teaspoon cream of tartar
Whipped Cream Frosting, see below
Fresh whipped cream, maraschino cherries with stems and freshly grated chocolate

WHIPPED CREAM FROSTING

Great on a Chocolate Mousse Cake or any cake!

In a small bowl, beat the cream until soft peaks form. Add the sugar and vanilla and beat until stiff.

1 cup whipping cream
⅓ cup powdered sugar
1 teaspoon vanilla

OLD-FASHIONED CHOCOLATE CAKE

Groff's Farm has become famous for the chocolate cake and cracker pudding we have on the table to begin the meal. It is rich and moist and stays fresh for a few days.

Cream the sugar, butter and eggs until fluffy. Mix in the buttermilk. Combine the cocoa and coffee in a saucepan, adding the liquid very slowly to prevent lumping, then mix into the creamed mixture. Moisten the baking soda with the vinegar and stir in with the salt and vanilla. Gradually mix in the flour, beating until smooth. Pour into a greased and floured 13″ x 9″ cake pan. Bake in a preheated 350° F. oven for approximately 45 minutes. Cool. Ice with Caramel Icing, see Index, or your favorite icing.

2 cups brown sugar
½ cup butter
2 eggs
¾ cup buttermilk
½ cup cocoa
½ cup boiling hot, strong coffee
1 teaspoon baking soda
1 teaspoon cider vinegar
½ teaspoon salt
1 teaspoon vanilla
2½ cups sifted all-purpose flour

WHITE CAKE

Cream butter and sugar in mixing bowl until fluffy. Gradually beat in the eggs. Sift together the flour, baking powder and salt. Stir in the flour mixture alternately with the milk, water, vanilla and lemon extracts into the sugar mixture. Fold in stiffly beaten egg whites. Pour the batter into 2 greased and floured 9″ layer pans. Bake in a preheated 350° F. oven for 35 minutes until it pulls away from the sides of the pans. Cool and frost with your favorite frosting, or with Boiled Frosting, see below.

Makes a 2 layer cake

- 2 cups granulated sugar
- ½ cup butter
- ½ cup vegetable shortening
- 3¼ cups cake flour, sifted
- 4¼ teaspoons baking powder
- 1 teaspoon salt
- 1 cup milk
- ⅓ cup water
- 1 teaspoon vanilla extract
- 1 teaspoon lemon extract
- 6 egg whites, stiffly beaten

BOILED FROSTING

In a small heavy saucepan, combine the sugar, water and cream of tartar. Stir and bring to a boil until it registers 242° F. on a candy thermometer. Meanwhile, beat the egg whites in a bowl until they hold soft peaks. Beat in 3 Tablespoons of the hot syrup, gradually by tablespoons. Pour the hot syrup slowly over the egg whites, beating steadily until the frosting stands in soft peaks. Add the vanilla and continue to beat until stiff enough to frost the cake. If frosting tends to become sugary, add a little lemon juice.

- 1½ cups granulated sugar
- ½ cup water
- ⅛ teaspoon cream of tartar
- 2 egg whites
- ½ teaspoon vanilla extract

MOTHER'S WHITE CAKE

This may be used as a 9" layer cake or a 9" x 13" cake for easier preparation.

In a large mixing bowl, cream the shortening and sugar until light and fluffy. Sift the flour, salt and baking powder in double sifter. Add the flour mixture alternately with the milk and vanilla, mixing thoroughly. Whip the egg whites until stiff and fold into the mixture. Pour into two greased 9" layer cake pans or one 9" x 13" pan. Bake in preheated 350° F. oven for 30 minutes. Cool and spread with icing.

⅔ cup shortening
1½ cups granulated sugar
2½ cups cake flour
½ teaspoon salt
3½ teaspoons baking powder
¾ cup milk
1 teaspoon vanilla
4 egg whites
Caramel Icing (see below)

VARIATION

Omit icing and use with fresh fruit instead of sponge cake.

CARAMEL ICING

Melt butter in a saucepan. Add the brown sugar and boil over low heat for 2 minutes, stirring constantly. Add milk and salt and stir until it comes to a full boil. Remove from heat and cool until lukewarm. Gradually beat in the confectioners' sugar, beating until the icing is thick enough to spread.

½ cup butter
1 cup brown sugar
¼ cup evaporated milk
◆ Pinch of salt
1¾ to 2 cups confectioners' sugar (enough for a spreading consistency)

DEVIL'S FOOD CAKE

Cream the sugars, salt, eggs, cocoa and shortening in mixing bowl until fluffy. Gradually add the sour cream, flour and vanilla. Dissolve baking soda in hot water or coffee and add to the above mixture, mixing until blended. Pour into greased 9″ x 13″ cake pan and bake in preheated 300° F. oven for 60 minutes. Top with your favorite icing or sprinkle with powdered sugar.

1 cup brown sugar
1 cup granulated sugar
◆ Pinch of salt
2 eggs
⅓ cup cocoa
½ cup vegetable shortening
½ cup sour cream
1 teaspoon vanilla
2 cups cake flour
1 cup hot water or coffee
1 teaspoon baking soda

BUTTER SPONGE CAKE

Grace Ross, a valued customer and fan, gave us this recipe which I consider a basic. You may use it as a cake, or under fresh fruit as a light shortcake. Save the egg whites for meringue to "fancy" any other fruit pie or pudding you may be making.

In large mixing bowl, beat the egg yolks and sugar until light and fluffy. Add slightly cooled milk and vanilla. Sift flour and baking powder and fold in alternately with melted butter until mixed thoroughly. Bake in two 8″ square pans in preheated 350° F. oven for 30 to 40 minutes. Test with toothpick inserted. When toothpick comes out clean, the cake is done. Serve plain or with Butter Frosting.

11	egg yolks
2	cups granulated sugar
1	cup milk, scalded
1	teaspoon vanilla
2¼	cups cake flour
2	teaspoons baking powder
½	cup melted butter (¼ pound)

BUTTER FROSTING

Cream the butter in a small bowl until soft. Add the cream, sugar and vanilla. Beat until smooth and creamy. Spread on the cake.

For Chocolate Icing melt a 1 ounce square of chocolate over very low heat and add it to the above mixture, or use 2 Tablespoons cocoa. Add more cream for the desired consistency. This should be enough for a 2-layer cake.

3	Tablespoons butter
1	Tablespoon cream
1½	cups confectioners sugar
½	teaspoon vanilla

APPLE BUTTER CAKE

Cream together the shortening and sugar. Beat in the eggs, one at a time. Beat until light and fluffy. Stir in 1¼ cups of the apple butter. Sift together the flour, baking powder, soda, salt, cinnamon and nutmeg. Add dry ingredients to the creamed mixture alternately with the milk. Turn into two greased and floured 9″ x 1½″ round pans. Bake in a preheated 350° F. oven for 30 to 35 minutes. Cool for 10 minutes. Remove from pans and cool thoroughly. Spread bottom layer of the cooled cake with ¼ cup of apple butter and evenly cover it with frosting. Cover with the top layer. Frost the cake and swirl the remaining ¼ cup of apple butter onto the frosted top to give a marbled effect. Garnish the sides of the cake with wedges of apple if desired.

HINT: To sour milk, measure 1 Tablespoon vinegar or lemon juice into a cup and add milk to measure 1 cup. Stir. The milk will sour and thicken.

½ cup shortening
1 cup sugar
3 eggs
1¼ cups apple butter
2½ cups sifted cake flour
3 teaspoons baking powder
½ teaspoon baking soda
½ teaspoon salt
1 teaspoon cinnamon
¼ teaspoon nutmeg
1 cup sour milk
½ cup apple butter for topping

CARROT CAKE

Cream shortening, add sugar, add eggs and beat well. Add the carrots. Mix and add sifted dry ingredients to creamed mixture alternately with milk and then add lemon extract. Bake in an 8″ x 11″ pan for about 45 minutes in a preheated 350° F. oven. Cool and ice with Cream Cheese Frosting, see below.

½ cup shortening
1¼ cups sugar
2 eggs
1½ cups carrot, grated
(4 medium carrots)
1½ cups flour
½ teaspoon salt
2 teaspoons ~~3 Tablespoons~~ baking powder
½ cup milk
1 teaspoon lemon extract

CREAM CHEESE FROSTING

Cream all of the above ingredients together until smooth.

6 ounces cream cheese
¼ pound butter
2 cups confectioners sugar
1 Tablespoon vanilla

ELLEN ENGEL'S CHEESECAKE

Grease a 10″ springform pan and dust with a mixture of crumbs, sugar and cinnamon. Stir and mash the cream cheese and beat in the sugar. Add the egg yolks, sour cream, vanilla and lemon juice and beat thoroughly. Beat the egg whites until stiff and fold into cheese mixture. Pour into pan and bake in a preheated 350° F. oven for 1 hour. Turn off the heat and leave the cake in the oven 1 hour longer, with door closed. Open door and leave cake in the oven with the door open for 30 minutes. Chill overnight and top with your favorite topping. It's especially good with Sour Cherry Topping.

Fine bread crumbs, sugar and cinnamon for dusting pan
3 8 ounce packages of cream cheese
1 cup sugar
6 eggs, separated
1 pint sour cream
2 teaspoons vanilla
1 teaspoon fresh lemon juice

SOUR CHERRY TOPPING

Drain the cherries and reserve the liquid. Mix the sugar and cornstarch and stir in the liquid. Cook, stirring constantly until the mixture thickens and boils. Boil and stir one minute. Remove from heat and stir in the butter, flavoring, coloring and the cherries. Cool thoroughly and spread on the top of Cheesecake or Sponge Cake.

1 pound can sour cherries
1 cup combined cherry liquid plus water
½ cup sugar
2 Tablespoons cornstarch
1 Tablespoon butter
½ teaspoon almond flavoring
◆ Few drops red food coloring

PEACH SOUR CREAM PIE

Place the sour cream in a bowl. Mix the sugar, salt and flour together and add to the sour cream. Add the eggs one at a time, beating thoroughly after each egg until the batter is smooth and creamy. Pour into the pie shell. Drain peaches and place cut side down in the mixture. Sprinkle cinnamon on top of the pie. Bake in a preheated 450° F. oven for 10 minutes, then decrease the heat to 350° and continue baking until the cream is thick and doesn't stick to a knife inserted into the middle. This should take another 35 to 40 minutes or until the knife comes out clean.

1 pint sour cream
1 cup sugar
◆ Dash of salt
1 teaspoon flour
3 eggs
6 to 8 canned peach halves
◆ Dash of cinnamon
1 9" unbaked pie shell

PEANUT BUTTER PIE

With a prepared pie shell, this only takes a few minutes to make and tastes great!

Cream peanut butter, sugar and milk in a large mixing bowl. Whip cream and fold into peanut butter mixture. When mixed well, pour into baked pie shell. Chill several hours. Garnish with peanuts, chopped or whole.

NOTE: Non-dairy whipped cream may be used as a substitute for cream. You may also use chunky peanut butter.

1 baked 9" pie shell
1 cup creamy peanut butter
½ cup superfine sugar
6 Tablespoons half-and-half or milk
1 cup heavy cream, whipped until stiff
Peanuts for garnish

BASIC PIE DOUGH

Use pastry cutter to cut the lard and butter into the salt and flour until they are fine crumbs. Carefully drip the ice water over the crumbs with one hand while tossing the crumbs lightly with the other. Use only enough water to hold the dough together. Be sure the water is sprinkled evenly over the flour mixture. As the dough becomes moist, gently press it to the sides of the bowl. The less the dough is handled after it is moistened, the flakier it will be. Put the dough on a generously floured board or counter. Gently pat it into a ball. Flatten the ball lightly, and pat the edges so there are no rough dry sides. Roll the dough until it is ⅛″ thick, moving the rolling pin in one direction, then in another. If the circle is not quite round, continue to roll out until it is. When the circle of dough is rounded, cut it 1″ larger than your pie pan. Put the dough around the rolling pin and slide it into the pie pan, cutting off any excess dough. Crimp, or flute, the edges unless there is a top crust. The trimmings may be used to make patty shells, or tart shells.

Makes two 9″ pie shells

NOTE: Only dampen as many crumbs as are needed for crust. Save the rest in a refrigerated container, adding the water when needed. I keep a gallon container filled with crumbs ready, to make into a pie shell at a moment's notice by adding ice water. Usually the amount of crumbs held in both hands is enough for 1 crust.

½   **cup lard or vegetable shortening**
¼   **cup butter**
¾   **teaspoon salt**
2½ **cups all-purpose flour**
⅓   **cup ice water, approximately**

APPLE PIE WITH CARAMEL CRUMB TOPPING

Roll out the pastry and fit in a 9″ pie pan. Combine the sugar, flour, cinnamon, nutmeg and salt in a bowl. Gradually add the light cream. Combine the sugar mixture with the sliced apples and put in the pie shell. Dot with butter. Press the crumbs for 1 pie in an ungreased pan and bake in a preheated 400° F. oven until golden brown, 8 to 10 minutes. Cool and crumble with a fork. Decrease the oven to 375° and bake the apple pie for 30 minutes or more until the apples are soft and the crust is golden brown. Heat the caramels and milk in a saucepan over low heat until smooth, stirring often. Pour the mixture over the apples and top with the recipe of crumbs. Bake for five minutes, or until the caramel bubbles through the crumbs. Cool before serving.

Pastry for 1 9″ pie crust
- 3½ cups peeled, cored and sliced apples
- ¾ cup granulated sugar
- 3 Tablespoons flour
- ½ teaspoon cinnamon
- ◆ Dash of nutmeg
- ¼ teaspoon salt
- ⅓ cup light cream or milk
- 2 Tablespoons butter
- 1 pound bag of vanilla caramels
- ½ cup milk

Pie Crumb Topping for 1 pie

CRUMB TOPPING FOR PIES

Combine the flour, sugar, butter and salt in a mixing bowl. Cut with a pastry cutter or with your hands until crumbs are fine. Put on top of fruit.

This recipe may be stored in refrigerator, using enough to cover ½″ thick on each pie.

- ¾ cup flour
- ¼ cup granulated sugar
- ¼ cup butter
- ◆ Pinch salt

BLACK RASPBERRY CRUMB PIE

Freeze the fresh berries in season, dry, then rinse them as you remove them from the freezer. This keeps them from getting freezer burn.

In a saucepan, dissolve the arrowroot in the water. Add sugar and mix well. Bring to a boil, stirring until sugar is dissolved and glaze slightly thickened. Arrowroot is expensive, but it makes a much clearer, finer glaze than cornstarch, which tends to be gummy. Remove from heat and stir in nutmeg. Fold in the berries. Pour the mixture into an unbaked 9″ pie shell and sprinkle with a ½″ thick layer of crumb topping. Bake in a 350° F. oven for 45 minutes. Serve warm or cold, but not straight from the oven or the pie will be hard to cut.

1 unbaked 9″ pie shell
3 Tablespoons arrowroot (may substitute cornstarch)
½ cup water
1 cup sugar
♦ Dash of nutmeg
2½ cups black raspberries
   Crumb Topping, see Index

CHOCOLATE WALNUT PIE

Here's another Cameron Estate specialty.

Cream sugar, cornstarch and eggs in mixing bowl until fluffy. Add syrup, butter and chocolate, blending thoroughly. Add vanilla. Use half the nuts in each pie shell and pour half the mixture over the nuts. Bake in preheated 300° F. oven for one hour.

2 unbaked 9″ pie shells
1 cup granulated sugar
1 Tablespoon cornstarch
4 eggs, lightly beaten
2 cups golden syrup or molasses
2 Tablespoons melted butter
2 squares unsweetened chocolate, melted
1 Tablespoon vanilla
2 cups whole or broken English walnuts, not chopped

AMISH VANILLA PIE

This is very much like a pecan pie without the pecans.

In a 1 quart saucepan, combine the molasses, sugar, egg and flour and mix well. Gradually add the hot water. Cook over medium heat until thickened, stirring constantly. Remove from heat and add the vanilla. Cool and pour into the unbaked pie shells. To make the crumb topping, mix all the topping ingredients together in a large bowl using a pastry cutter or mix by hand. Combine until the crumbs are fine. Divide in half, using half on each pie. Bake in a preheated 375° F. oven for 10 minutes, then reduce heat to 350° and bake 30 minutes longer until the center of the pie is firm.

2 unbaked 9" pie shells

BOTTOM
1 cup golden table molasses or barrel molasses, not baking molasses
½ cup sugar
1 egg, slightly beaten
2 Tablespoons flour
2 cups hot water
1 teaspoon vanilla extract

CRUMB TOPPING
1 cup sugar
½ cup butter
½ teaspoon baking soda
½ teaspoon cream of tartar
2 cups flour

FUNNY PIE

I elevated the ordinary funny pie recipe to meet the standards of CHOCOLATIER Magazine. Now we have a real winner! Some have called it sinful.

For bottom, stir the sugar, salt and cocoa together in a saucepan. Slowly add the hot water and chocolate liqueur, blending until smooth. Bring to a boil and simmer for 5 minutes. Remove from heat and add the vanilla and almonds. Cool while preparing the topping. Cream the butter and sugar in a mixing bowl. Beat in the eggs, one at a time. Sift the flour, salt and baking powder into another bowl. Gradually beat into the creamed mixture, alternating with the milk and liqueur, until smooth. Add the vanilla and blend. Pour the cooled liquid bottom mixture into the unbaked pie shells. Drop the batter evenly over it. Sprinkle the roasted almonds over the top. Bake in a pre-heated 375° F. oven for 50 to 60 minutes until the filling is firm when the pie pans are moved.

2 unbaked pie shells

LIQUID BOTTOM MIXTURE

- 1 cup granulated sugar
- ½ teaspoon salt
- ½ cup cocoa
- ½ cup roasted almonds, coarsely chopped
- ½ cup hot water
- ½ cup chocolate liquour
- 1 teaspoon vanilla

BATTER FOR TOPPING

- ½ cup butter, room temperature
- 2 cups granulated sugar
- 2 eggs
- 2 cups flour
- ½ teaspoon salt
- 2 teaspoons baking powder
- ½ cup milk
- ½ cup chocolate liquour
- ½ teaspoon vanilla
- ½ cup roasted almonds, coarsely chopped

SHOOFLY PIE

Combine the flour, brown sugar, and shortening in a bowl and cut with a pastry blender or rub with your fingers until it forms fine crumbs. Put the unbaked pie shell in a preheated oven at 350° F. for about 5 minutes to prevent the bottom from getting soggy. Dissolve the soda in the boiling water in a bowl. Add the molasses and salt and stir to blend well. Pour liquid mixture into the unbaked pie shell and sprinkle evenly with crumb topping. Bake in a preheated 375° F. oven for 10 minutes. Reduce the temperature to 350° and bake for 30 minutes longer, or until set (when the pie is given a gentle shake, the top should remain firm). Serve warm with whipped cream or ice cream.

CRUMB TOPPING
1 cup unsifted flour
½ cup light brown sugar
¼ cup vegetable shortening

LIQUID BOTTOM
1 teaspoon baking soda
1 cup boiling water
1 cup golden table molasses
¼ teaspoon salt
9" unbaked pie shell

PUMPKIN-MAPLE PIE

Blend together the sugar, syrup, cinnamon, allspice, nutmeg, and salt with the eggs. Stir in the pumpkin and milk. Pour ingredients into the pie shell and bake in a preheated 450° F. oven for 15 minutes, then at 300° F. for another 25 to 30 minutes. Do the knife test an inch in from the rim of the crust. If it comes out clean, it's done. Before serving the cooled pie, whip the cream, adding the syrup and vanilla, and top each portion with a dollop of the cream.

½ cup brown sugar, packed
¼ cup maple syrup
½ teaspoon cinnamon
½ teaspoon allspice
½ teaspoon nutmeg
½ teaspoon salt
3 eggs, lightly beaten
16 ounce can pumpkin
1¼ cups evaporated milk
9" unbaked pie shell, see Index
½ cup heavy cream
1 to 2 Tablespoons of maple syrup
1 teaspoon vanilla

DUTCH PEAR PIE

Sift together the flour and sugar and stir in the lemon juice, then the cream. Mix until smooth. Cut the pears in small pieces and add to the creamed mixture. Pour into an unbaked pie shell and sprinkle with the sugar and cinnamon. Bake in a preheated 425° F. oven for 45 to 50 minutes. Cool until set.

¼ cup flour
½ cup sugar
1 Tablespoon lemon juice
1 cup heavy cream
4 to 5 large fresh pears or 8 canned pear halves
1 Tablespoon sugar
¼ teaspoon cinnamon
Pie shell, see Index

COOKIES AND CANDY PIE

If you don't REALLY like chocolate, don't try this pie!

Place the milk and marshmallows in the top half of a double boiler and stir occasionally until melted. Cool slightly and add chocolate bars, broken into small pieces. Add the flavoring and stir until the chocolate is melted. Let stand until cool and thick. Add the whipped cream and fold in thoroughly. Pour into the baked shell and set. Serve with additional whipped cream and a few toasted almonds.

½ cup milk
20 large marshmallows
6 small chocolate bars with almonds
¼ teaspoon almond extract
1 pint cream, whipped
¾ cup slivered toasted almonds
Chocolate Pie Shell or regular pie crust, see below

CHOCOLATE PIE SHELL

Melt the butter and mix in a bowl with the crushed cookies. Blend thoroughly and firmly press into a pie plate. Bake in a preheated 350° F. oven for 10 to 12 minutes. Be careful about the timing. The chocolate darkens quickly.

½ cup unsalted butter
8½ ounce box of chocolate wafer cookies, crushed, approximately 40, 2" cookies

SUGAR CREAM PIE

For years cooks have made something out of almost nothing. One good example is this pie. In some areas it's known as Sugar Cream, in others it's a Johnny Pie. These were originally made for the children out of the scraps of pie dough pressed into tart pans and filled with milk and sugar, etc. The filling was so thin that people were accused of eating pie with nothing in it.

In a bowl, lightly whip the flour and sugar into the cream and milk. Pour into an unbaked pie shell that has foil wrapped over the crust edge. The pie will take awhile to bake and this will help the crust from getting too dark. Dot the top of the mixture with the butter cut into three pieces and sprinkle with the cinnamon and nutmeg. Bake in a preheated 350° F. oven for one hour. Remove the foil for the last 15 minutes of the baking time. The filling will still shake and look gooey, but it will set up as it cools. The flavor is best when served slightly warm.

- 1 cup sugar
- ⅓ cup flour
- 1 cup heavy cream
- 1½ cups of milk
- 1 Tablespoon butter
- ◆ Dash of cinnamon
- ◆ Dash of nutmeg
- 9" pie crust, see Index

APPLE COOKIES

In a bowl sift the flour, soda, salt and spices. Cream the butter and sugar. Add egg and milk and beat until smooth. Gradually stir in the sifted mixture and fold in the apples, raisins and nuts. Drop by teaspoon full on greased cookie sheet. Bake in a preheated 375° F. oven for 10 minutes.

- 2 cups flour
- 1 teaspoon baking soda
- ½ teaspoon salt
- 1 teaspoon cinnamon
- 1 teaspoon cloves
- 1 teaspoon nutmeg
- ½ cup butter
- 1⅓ cups brown sugar
- 1 egg
- ¼ cup milk
- 1 cup apple, chopped
- 1 cup raisins
- 1 cup pecans, chopped

CRACKER PUDDING

Heat the milk. Beat the egg yolks and sugar until frothy and light. Add to the hot milk, and stir in the crackers and coconut. Cook over medium heat until thick. Remove from heat. Stiffly beat the egg whites and fold in with the vanilla. Serve cool or cold.

Beat the egg whites with the cream of tartar to the soft-peak stage. Gradually beat in the 4 Tablespoons sugar and continue beating until stiff and glossy. Pile this meringue lightly over the cracker pudding and bake in a 350° F. oven until meringue is golden brown.

1 quart milk
2 eggs, separated
2/3 cup granulated sugar
2 cups broken saltine crackers
1 cup grated coconut, medium shred
1 teaspoon vanilla

MERINGUE

3 egg whites
1/4 teaspoon cream of tartar
4 Tablespoons sugar

NEIGHBORS DELIGHT

This is an excellent dessert to have in the freezer for last minute entertaining.

In mixing bowl, cream the sugar and egg yolks until fluffy. Gradually add the milk and place in heavy 2 quart sauce pan. Bring to a boil on medium heat and cook until slightly thickened, stirring constantly, approximately 5 minutes. Remove from heat and stir in jello. Cool. When cool, add drained pineapple. Whip the cream to soft peaks. Fold in the stiffly beaten egg whites and whipped cream. Cut half the cake in thin slices to cover bottom of 9″ × 13″ cake pan. Pour half the whipped mixture over cake. Sprinkle half the cherries on top. Cut the other half of cake in thin slices and place on top of mixture. Add remaining whipped mixture and cherries and freeze for at least 8 hours before serving. Remove from freezer 30 minutes before serving.

1 angel food cake
1 cup granulated sugar
2 egg yolks, save whites for later
2 cups milk
1 3 ounce package lemon jello
1 cup crushed pineapple, drained
2 egg whites, stiffly beaten
2 cups whipping cream
1 cup maraschino cherry halves

CHOCOLATE CARAMELS

Combine the sugar, syrup, butter, chocolate and milk in a heavy saucepan and cook until the mixture reaches 248° F. on a candy thermometer. The stove should be set so that the syrup boils slowly. Stir the mixture constantly. When the medium hard ball stage is reached, remove from heat, add the vanilla and pour into a buttered 8″ square pan or ovenproof dish. Cool thoroughly before cutting.

3 cups sugar
1 cup golden molasses
1 cup butter
¼ pound milk chocolate
1 cup milk
1 teaspoon vanilla

VANILLA CARAMELS

Combine the sugar, syrup and butter in a heavy saucepan and boil for 15 minutes, stirring constantly with a wooden spoon. Add the milk and boil to the medium hard ball stage on a candy thermometer, around 248° F. Continue stirring the whole time the syrup is cooking. If you don't have a thermometer, drop a little syrup, about ½ teaspoon, into a cup of very cold water to see if it's the desired firmness. It takes awhile for the temperature to reach the medium hard stage, then it can jump quickly and scorch, so be very careful. Remove from heat and add nuts if desired and the vanilla. Pour into a buttered 8″ × 8″ dish and let cool thoroughly before cutting.

2 cups sugar
1 cup golden molasses
½ cup butter
1 cup milk
1 cup nut meats, chopped
1 teaspoon vanilla

CURRANT-PECAN TARTS

Cut the butter into the flour. Combine the egg yolk with the sour cream and blend into the flour mixture. Chill the dough overnight. It will seem very sticky, but will be ready to work in the morning. Roll the dough very thin on a floured surface and cut into circles slightly larger than a muffin cup. Press into greased cups. Fill ⅓ full with the tart mixture. Bake in a preheated 400° F. oven for 10–12 minutes. Don't overbake. Cool on racks. This is equally good as a pie.

Makes 12 tarts

SOUR CREAM PASTRY

- 1 cup butter
- 2 cups flour
- 1 egg yolk
- ½ cup sour cream

TART MIXTURE

- 2 Tablespoon butter, melted
- 1 cup brown sugar
- 1½ cups currants or raisins
- 1–2 eggs, beaten
- 1 teaspoon vanilla
- 1 cup chopped pecans
- 2 Tablespoons milk

CASHEW BRITTLE

Combine sugar, syrup and water together in a deep, heavy saucepan and bring to a boil. Insert candy thermometer and cook on medium heat to hard ball stage (250° F.), stirring frequently. Add the nuts and continue to boil to 300° F., stirring constantly. Keep a close eye on the syrup temperature as it takes quite a while to reach the 290° F. mark, then all of a sudden it spurts to 300° F. and it is finished. Stir in the soda and pour onto a buttered cookie sheet. Break when cool.

VARIATION

Peanuts may be substituted.

- 2 cups granulated sugar
- 1 cup white corn syrup
- ½ cup water
- 3 cups raw, unsalted cashews
- 2 teaspoons soda

NUT COOKIES

In a mixing bowl, combine the sugar, shortening mixture and eggs and blend thoroughly. Sift the flour and soda together and add them to the mixture a little at a time until well blended. Stir in the vanilla and form the dough into a roll. Place the dough on plastic wrap and roll up tightly. Put in the freezer for a couple of hours. Unwrap, slice thin, and bake in a preheated 350° F. oven for 8 to 10 minutes. The cookies will be light in color but will crisp as they cool.

2   cups brown sugar
¾   cup butter and shortening
2   eggs
3 to 3½   cups flour
1   teaspoon soda
1   teaspoon vanilla
1   cup nut meats, chopped

MAMMY'S MOLASSES COOKIES

Mammy Wise was born into a family of canal operators, between Port Trevorten and Millersburg, Pennsylvania. This recipe and her Applesauce Cookies were baked in a coal stove oven year-round to the delight of her grandchildren.

Preheat oven to 350° F. Mix together the shortening, sugar, molasses and milk. Place all remaining dry ingredients in a separate bowl and blend them together: the soda, ginger, cinnamon, salt, cloves, nutmeg and flour. Add the dry ingredients to the liquid mixture. It should make a stiff, moist batter. If it is too moist, add a very small amount of flour. When thoroughly blended, roll out and cut with a cup or a cookie cutter. Bake for 10 to 12 minutes.

Makes 2 dozen cookies.

1   cup soft shortening
1   cup granulated sugar
1   cup light molasses
1   cup sour milk
3   teaspoons baking soda
2   teaspoons ginger
2   teaspoons cinnamon
1   teaspoon salt
½   teaspoon ground cloves
½   teaspoon ground nutmeg
4   cups flour

MAMMY'S APPLESAUCE COOKIES

Preheat oven to 375° F. Mix together the shortening, brown sugar and egg. Stir in the applesauce. Sift together the flour, baking soda, salt, cinnamon, and cloves. Add to liquid mixture. Add raisins and/or black walnuts if desired. Drop onto cookie sheet and bake for 10 to 12 minutes.

Makes 3½ dozen cookies.

¾ cup soft shortening
1 cup brown sugar
1 egg
¾ cup applesauce
2¼ cups sifted flour
½ teaspoon baking soda
½ teaspoon salt
¾ teaspoon cinnamon
¼ teaspoon ground cloves
1 cup of seedless raisins (optional)
½ cup nuts, black walnuts (optional)

PUMPKIN BARS

In a mixing bowl, combine the sugar, flour, pumpkin, oil, eggs, baking powder, soda, cinnamon, and salt and beat thoroughly. Pour into a greased jelly roll pan, 15½″ × 10½″, or a cookie sheet with sides. Bake in a preheated 350° F. oven for 25 to 35 minutes. Cool and frost with Cream Cheese Icing and cut into bars before removing from the pan.

2 cups sugar
2 cups flour
16 ounce can of pumpkin
1 cup oil
4 eggs
2 teaspoons baking powder
1 teaspoon soda
1 teaspoon cinnamon
½ teaspoon salt
Cream Cheese Icing, see Index

MORAVIAN SUGAR CAKE

In every Moravian community there is a fierce competition for the "best" Moravian sugar cake. Many of the folks will not part with their winner, but the Regennas family of Lititz (famous for their clear toy candy shop) are happy to share this with us. I always had the children help me make this cake because they loved to take their little fingers and push the holes in the top.

To proof the yeast, add a pinch of sugar to the yeast in warm water. If it foams, it is good. Hot liquid will kill the yeast action, thus the lukewarm water. In large mixing bowl, cream the eggs, sugar and shortening till smooth. Gradually add warm milk and mashed potatoes, stirring a bit, then add the yeast, mixing well. Add flour, a cup at a time, until dough is stiff enough to turn out on a floured board. Knead until dough is soft and spongy, about 10 to 15 minutes by hand or if done in a food processor, mix until it forms a ball. Place in large greased bowl in a draft-free warm place and cover with damp towel. Let dough double in size, approximately 2 to 3 hours, punch down and divide dough. Place in greased pie pans or large cookie sheets, covered, and let double in size again, approximately 1½ hours. Spread melted butter on top of cakes, punching holes in dough about 1 inch apart with fingers. Be careful not to punch to the bottom of the pan, but only halfway down. Mix the topping thoroughly and pour into the holes in the dough. Sprinkle remaining crumbs over top and sprinkle with cinnamon. Bake in a preheated 350° F. oven for 20 minutes or until golden and fully baked on the bottom. Serve warm with coffee or tea or as a dessert.

1 package (1 Tablespoon) dry yeast, dissolved in ½ cup lukewarm water
2 eggs
½ cup sugar
⅔ cup shortening
1 cup hot riced or mashed potatoes (if using instant, use water for liquid and do not add salt)
1 cup scalded milk, cooled to warm
1½ teaspoons salt
6 to 7 cups all purpose flour
½ cup melted butter

TOPPING

2 pounds light brown sugar
½ cup flour
4 Tablespoons butter
Sprinkle with cinnamon

ACKNOWLEDGMENTS

A big thank you to each friend listed below:

Diane Stonebeck, a super creative writer, for the Up-Home Down-Home introduction and who has translated my thoughts and memories in the narratives preceding each chapter.

Barb Adams for the continued support, hard work and long hours to bring this together.

Tom and Cheryl Wise for their patience and wisdom.

Our Chefs, managers and staff of our Groff's Farm Restaurant and Cameron Estate Inn. I really appreciate each one.

Sharron Quay, for the fine design work with Flat Tulip Studio.

Frank Costello and R.R. Donnelley & Sons Company.

Donna Fahnestock for proofreading and paste-up.

Chris Kunzler, Jr. and the great people of Kunzler and Company, Inc.

The Monteith Portrait Studio and Gallery, Lancaster, Pennsylvania, for the picture on the rear dust cover.

Our valued customers through the years who continue to support us with your presence and suggestions for the future publications.

Steven Friesen, Director, Hans Herr House, for sharing your love of history. Your patience and sense of humor while we worked was refreshing.

The illustrations, based on the Hans Herr House, symbolize the heritage of Betty Groff, a tenth generation descendant of Hans Herr. We wish to thank the Hans Herr Museum for their gracious cooperation in the development of these pictures.

The Hans Herr House Museum, 2215 Mill Stream Road, Lancaster, Pa. 17602 is open for visitors. Hours are 9 A.M. to 4 P.M. daily, Mondays through Saturdays. Closed Sundays, Thanksgiving, Christmas and January 1 through March 31.

For additional copies, please check your local bookstore or write to:

Pond Press Publishers
650 Pinkerton Road
Mount Joy, Pennsylvania, 17552

or call: 717-653-1115 for additional information.

Full color art seen on chapter pages is available for purchase as signed prints. For a colored brochure containing prices and more information, write Pond Press.

Index

Notes

Notes

Notes

Notes